IT GOVERNANCE IN HOSPITALS AND HEALTH SYSTEMS

Roger Kropf, PhD, and Guy Scalzi, MBA

CRC Press
Taylor & Francis Group
6000 Broken Sound Parkway NW, Suite 300
Boca Raton, FL 33487-2742

Visit the Taylor & Francis Web site at
http://www.taylorandfrancis.com

and the CRC Press Web site at
http://www.crcpress.com

About the Authors

Roger Kropf, PhD, is a Professor in the Health Policy and Management Program at New York University's Robert F. Wagner Graduate School of Public Service. Dr. Kropf has also been a Visiting Professor since 1997 at the University of Colorado Denver Business School, where he teaches in the Executive MBA Program in Health Administration. He teaches a course on healthcare management information systems at both universities. Dr. Kropf is the author of three books on the application of information systems to healthcare management. *Strategic Analysis for Hospital Management* was written with James Greenberg, PhD, and published by Aspen Systems in 1984. *Service Excellence in Health Care through the Use of Computers* was published by the American College of Healthcare Executives in 1990. *Making Information Technology Work: Maximizing the Benefits for Health Care Organizations* was written with Guy Scalzi and published by Health Forum/AHA Press in 2007. More information is available at www.nyu.edu/classes/kropf.

Guy Scalzi, MBA, is a principal in Aspen Advisors, a professional services firm that works with healthcare organizations to enhance processes and streamline operations through the strategic and effective use of technology. He was previously Executive Vice President of Veloz Global Solutions, a Business Intelligence Company. From 1999 to 2006, he was Senior Vice President and Managing Director of FCG's Management Services business. Mr. Scalzi has held the position of Chief Information Officer (CIO) at New York-Presbyterian Hospital, New York/Cornell Medical Center and the Hospital for Joint Diseases, a division of New York University Medical Center. In 1985, he became one of the founders of a software development company, DataEase International, which developed and sold database software to hospitals throughout North America, Europe, Asia and South America. He also served as a hospital administrator in New York City at St. Vincent's Medical Center, Bellevue Hospital and Montefiore/Einstein Medical Center.

Dedication

To Marcia and Claudia

Acknowledgments

We want to thank the people who took time out of their busy lives to help us develop case studies for the book:

- Cathy Bruno, Chief Information Officer, Eastern Maine Healthcare Systems, Brewer, Maine
- Jim Burton, Senior Vice President and Chief Information Officer, East Jefferson General Hospital, Metairie, Louisiana
- Deborah Gash, Vice President and Chief Information Officer, Saint Luke's Health System, Kansas City, Missouri

We also want to thank the managers and clinicians at those three organizations for agreeing to be interviewed and sharing their thoughts and experiences on the IT governance process.

And we would like to thank the chief information officers who agreed to be interviewed and gave us valuable insights into the governance process:

- David L. Miller, Vice Chancellor and Chief Information Officer, University of Arkansas for Medical Sciences, Little Rock, Arkansas
- Lynn H. Vogel, PhD, Vice President and Chief Information Officer, The University of Texas MD Anderson Cancer Center, Houston, Texas
- Eric Yablonka, Vice President and Chief Information Officer, University of Chicago Medical Center, Chicago, Illinois

Table of Contents

Foreword

By Joseph R. Swedish, President and CEO, Trinity Health

At Trinity Health, experience has taught us the tremendous value of and need for strong IT governance, having integrated the 20 markets in our national 10-state system into one clinical, financial and operational IT platform over the last 12 years. In *IT Governance in Hospitals and Health Systems*, Roger Kropf and Guy Scalzi take a straightforward and pragmatic approach to IT governance that will benefit many healthcare providers—particularly independent hospitals and smaller regional systems. Many in healthcare will be able to glean useful insights and apply the lessons learned through the examples cited in the book.

When Trinity Health set out in 1999 to create a single nationwide IT platform, our goal was to leverage an integrated system of information management to radically transform care delivery, increase patient safety and improve financial performance. We now know that clear focus is critical when developing an IT system, and a governance committee unquestionably provides the needed direction given the disruptive nature of workflow and the upheaval to the decision process.

As the authors make clear, an IT governance structure must prioritize projects, allocate funding and determine accountability that is often counter to the status quo. There are many other roles that IT governance plays, such as evaluating the performance of logistical support and developing policies for IT security and social media.

Health systems and hospitals should carefully consider the role that IT governance administers and include those elements in a committee charter to ensure authority, purpose of work and continuity. Clarity of expectations and accountability is essential to assure that the committee's work is valued guidance and, if necessary, mandates performance. Through our IT journey at Trinity Health, we discovered that to get the best return on our investment, the governance committee had to be flexible so that it could change course when wrong decisions were made, that not everyone would be happy with the change and that ultimately organizations have to "break glass" to transform the culture. As we have learned, culture transformation is often the elephant in the room and effective controls can tame the behaviors that frequently compromise the go-lives' ability to function as designed.

Roger and Guy have brought forward models for accelerated performance as organizations seek to transform the most complex aspect of their decision-making infrastructure. Indeed, it is my belief that how an organization operates its information management systems is directly correlated to how the organization makes decisions. It is abundantly clear when the ingredients offered to create an efficient and effective governance authority are imbedded in the process, the complex becomes manageable.

Preface

Good governance, when properly executed, provides project managers with a clear understanding of the priority of projects, the resources available and who is accountable for project implementation. This results in a portfolio of projects that moves the organization toward the achievement of a single, unified vision of how IT will develop. Good governance increases the support of key stakeholders by giving them a voice in formulating that vision. It increases the number of IT projects that support the strategy of a hospital or health system and are completed on time and on budget.

We are going to argue that not having an IT governance process, or having one that never seriously involves clinicians and other stakeholders, is a big mistake.

The emphasis on obtaining federal funds by meaningful use of a certified electronic health record (EHR) system may seem to reduce the importance of governance. Why have a governance process when we know what we have to do? But is that true? Is the entire IT strategy of your organization just meeting Meaningful Use requirements at each stage? IT strategy goes beyond implementing an EHR system. It includes integration across the continuum of care, patient engagement, patient portals, support of clinical care through improvements in clinical decision support, data storage, imaging and networking, and improvement of financial systems, security and disaster recovery. An IT governance process is needed for prioritization, gaining stakeholder support and ensuring that value is actually received.

If we have convinced you that a serious IT governance process is necessary, then this book will provide you with a step-by-step course of action that incorporates best practices.

Introduction

. . .gradually over a period of years, involving hundreds of conversations with managers and multiple research studies, we became convinced that IT governance is the most important factor in generating business value from IT.

—Peter Weill and Jeanne Ross,
MIT Sloan School of Management[1]

IT Governance in Hospitals and Health Systems describes how to create an information technology (IT) governance process that increases the number of IT projects supporting the strategy of a hospital or health system and are completed on time and on budget.

It defines and describes IT governance as it is currently practiced in leading healthcare organizations. Without a governance structure, IT at many hospitals and healthcare systems is a haphazard endeavor that typically results in late, over-budget projects and, ultimately, many disparate systems that do not function well together.

IT Governance in Hospitals and Health Systems defines IT governance and why it is important. It describes the components of IT governance and the keys to a successful governance process. Roles, responsibilities and committee structure are defined. Processes and workflows that lead to successful governance are described. The relationship of IT governance to project and portfolio management is explained. Also, in addition to the examples from hospitals and health systems that appear throughout the book, Chapters 6 through 8 present detailed case studies of effective IT governance.

Quick Start Guide to
IT Governance in Hospitals and Health Systems

IT governance is needed because there is an almost infinite need for IT and finite resources available to the organization. Chief information officers (CIOs) and their staffs cannot set priorities by themselves. Senior executives and the clinical staff need to be involved. Demand management and project prioritization are both essential. Results also need to be certified by an oversight group. They need to assure that the technology and processes work as planned and that most projects are completed on time and on budget.

What Are the Most Important Things to Do?

Defining the committee structure is essential. An IT governance or steering committee is needed, as well as advisory committees. Who will agree to participate and will they commit to the process? You need to identify senior managers and clinicians who are willing to dedicate the time, see committee membership as more than ceremonial and have the best interests of the whole institution in mind.

Create a Governance or Steering Committee. The governance or steering committee needs to govern all IT projects and be chaired by the CIO. The committee should include the chief financial officer (CFO) or another senior finance person and a top-level management person, preferably the chief operating officer (COO). Senior nursing leadership should also be on the committee, as well as a building services executive. Senior medical staff who are employed in administration and paid by the institution should be included, as well as independent physicians who admit patients.

Define a Governance Process. The governance committee reviews all proposals that have been thoroughly previewed by an advisory committee. There are typically three to four advisory committees; these include committees for clinical services, finance and ambulatory care. The advisory committees review proposals to determine their benefits and their likely return on investment. The governance committee then prioritizes the proposals for submission to the finance committee of the hospital's or health system's board of directors.

Validating each project, the governance committee determines whether it should be done now or put in a future year's budget. The committee also has a role in ensuring that each project is completed on time and on budget. Project management prepares both the budget and the time line, which then come to the governance committee for review and approval. Project management provides the committee with regular reports as the project progresses.

Major projects, such as an institution-wide EHR system, might have a different process. A subcommittee with much broader representation might be formed that includes, for example, representatives of the medical school and a faculty practice. Responsibilities of this committee go beyond IT to implementation, operations and benefit realization. This subcommittee reports to the governance committee.

Create Advisory Committees. Often, advisory committees originate projects as well as review those that are submitted to them. Representatives from the various departments will suggest new projects. Advisory committees provide an easily identified way to express concerns about existing systems. A system installed two years ago may not be functioning well, and advisory committees give staff an opportunity to present the issues. All committees should have a senior IT staff member. Typically, the IT person does not have a role in project management but can help validate and interpret the technology.

Define the Role of the Board. The board of a hospital or health system usually has a finance committee that approves budgets and projects. In smaller organizations, there may be at best one or two people on the board who understand IT projects and so the board relies heavily on the IT governance committee. In larger organizations, there may be board members who have in-depth IT knowledge and experience and have more independent views.

Define the Role of the CEO. The chief executive officer (CEO) should be a member of the governance committee but would not be expected to come to all meetings. Some CEOs choose to be involved only when the projects are large, expensive or controversial. Other CEOs review proposals when they come to the finance committee on which they serve. CEOs may choose to attend all meetings of the governance committee when there has been a history of significant problems, such as failed projects or financial losses.

Require Project Sponsors Who Are Accountable. Every project should have a business sponsor who is not part of IT. The only time a sponsor should be an IT staff member is when a project relates to IT operations or infrastructure. The business sponsor brings the project to the advisory committee, and the IT governance committee then follows it during implementation with the help of a project manager. Although the project manager monitors the project, it is the project sponsor who is accountable. For larger projects, the project sponsor provides the IT governance committee with a final report indicating whether the project was completed, whether completion was on time and on budget and what modifications were made. For the largest projects, the sponsor will return to the governance committee 6 to 18 months following completion to describe whether the project actually provided the benefits that were expected. This allows the committee to assess its own work.

Create a PMO or Hire a Project Manager. Larger organizations should have a project management office (PMO) that creates and disseminates project management procedures, assigns project managers to projects and prepares reports for the business sponsor and governance committee. Smaller organizations should hire or train staff to be project managers for IT projects. Those persons should have extensive project experience or be trained project managers (e.g., Project Management Professionals [PMPs] certified by the Project Management Institute [www.pmi.org]). Local colleges and universities may also offer training.

What Are the Keys to Success?

Communicate. The CEO needs to communicate the governance process to the organization. A charter should be prepared and widely disseminated from the CEO. The CEO communicates that the process must be followed and that projects are not to be submitted to the CEO or the board directly. Deadlines for submission to the advisory committees and the governance committee are defined.

Meet Regularly. The governance committee needs to meet regularly and follow the finance committee calendar for submission of proposals. Do not be afraid to cancel meetings when no decisions need to be made. Committee members will stop coming if they believe that they lack real authority and that meetings are just for updates or presentations. Meetings are for considering new projects, setting priorities and reviewing existing and completed projects.

Do Not Be Afraid to Rotate Members. Senior managers and clinicians do not have to serve on every committee for every term. Allow them to nominate others to the committee, but do not allow substitutions for individual meetings. Senior managers and clinicians must be able to say, however, that their nominees speak for them. For example, the medical director might appoint a medical department head to a committee. That person has to commit to serving for a specified term (e.g., a year). Members who cannot attend a meeting are not allowed to vote on that meeting's issues, nor are they allowed to send a substitute. Explaining the committee's tasks and processes to one-time attendees would waste too much time.

Do Not Allow Gaming. As stated earlier, the CEO needs to communicate that the process will be followed and that *no* IT project will be allowed to proceed unless it has gone through the governance process. Moreover, it should be impossible to skirt the governance process by breaking a project into pieces, each of which falls below the threshold for submission. To avoid this, the threshold for review can be set at a very low level (e.g., 80 hours of work for IT or $10,000).

Some project sponsors may also try to circumvent the governance process by underestimating their budgets. For example, they may include the cost of software but not the data conversion or hardware costs. To avoid this, the project managers in IT who review smaller projects need to carefully consider each proposal to identify needed components and a realistic budget. The facts of a proposal may be verified by speaking directly to vendors.

Have an Expedited Process for Smaller Projects. The governance committee should establish an expedited review process for smaller projects. Doing so will reduce the concern that the governance process will cause significant delays. It will also help to trim the workload created by setting thresholds low enough to discourage gaming. When an expedited small-project process is in place, the governance committee will not feel they are wasting time looking at insignificant projects.

Recognize the Importance of Good Staff Work. Staff are needed to support the process by thoroughly reviewing the projects. IT staff and the governance and advisory committees need to define the questions to be answered (e.g., what is the project's return on investment?) to avoid repeatedly returning proposals with requests for more information. If each proposal is expected to be accompanied by a completed form, then staff should ensure that each form is complete before it is sent to a committee. Minutes are important and should define all the actions that need to be taken after the meeting. The minutes need to be widely disseminated so that everybody knows what is being proposed and what has to be done.

Chapter 1

What Is IT Governance and Why Is It Important?

Definition of IT Governance

Weill and Ross define IT governance as "specifying the decision rights and account-ability framework to encourage desirable behavior in using IT"[2]:

> IT governance is not about making specific IT decisions. That is manage-ment. Rather, governance is about systematically determining who makes each type of decision (a decision right), who has input to a decision (an input right) and how these people (or groups) are held accountable for their role. Good IT governance draws on corporate governance principles to manage and use IT to achieve corporate performance goals.[3]

To do that requires the creation of a formal structure that includes defined roles, responsibilities and accountability for decisions.

> IT governance is "putting structure around how organizations align IT strategy with business strategy, ensuring that companies stay on track to achieve their strategies and goals, and implementing good ways to measure IT's performance. It makes sure that all stakeholders' interests are taken into account and that processes provide measurable results."[4]

IT governance includes a set of committees to involve stakeholders and defined pro-cesses for approving and managing IT projects.

Why Governance Is Important[5]

The business is changing rapidly. The pace of the change and the significance of the change in the next couple of years is breathtaking. Governance is more important now than ever. You need to have alignment. There needs to be ownership of the IT spending at the orga-nizational level. In governance, one size doesn't fit all. Your governance process will be evolving to stay in front of the changing marketplace. Use governance as one of your levers.
—Eric Yablonka, Vice President and Chief Information Officer,
University of Chicago Medical Center, Chicago, IL

Governance is an opportunity to educate the organization and drive more efficient use of resources and better decision making.
                              —David L. Miller, Vice Chancellor and Chief Information Officer,
                                   University of Arkansas for Medical Sciences, Little Rock, AR

The challenge is to control IT decision-making, yet empower different stakeholders to take responsibility for IT decisions.[6]

Governance for information technology is as important for a healthcare provider as it is for any discipline or organization. Without governance, some form of anarchy eventually results. In hospital IT departments, this takes the form of staff moving from crisis to crisis, only capable of responding to the loudest, most powerful voice, the most recent regulatory change, or the most serious emergency. There is no structure that sets priorities and plans workflow to allow the majority of staff to function in a stable and productive manner rather than just respond to emergencies. It becomes impossible to measure and track progress over time. The rest of the organization tends to view IT as out of control.

A governance structure leads IT planning efforts by setting priorities that are aligned with those of the organization. A senior-level IT governance committee whose members represent a broad range of interests within a hospital or group of hospitals becomes the focal point for all major IT requests. That group vets and prioritizes proposals and then sends them to the budget committee for funding. In some cases, the budget committee first gives IT a target capital amount, and the governance committee tries to select proposals whose total costs will not exceed that number.

IT leadership reports back to the governance committee with progress updates and issues lists for all funded projects. For example, the committee works closely with the project management office to address areas that require additional funding, people or senior management attention. Successful organizations have found that through this process, it is possible to maintain more than 90% of projects on time and on budget.

Shaping Expectations, Standardizing Processes and Conferring Legitimacy on Decisions

The governance process shapes expectations so that the clinical or business sponsors of an IT project, as well as IT staff, understand what benefits should be achieved and what responsibilities each has for project completion and achievement of benefits. The governance process confers legitimacy on decisions so that, for example, project selection is viewed as impartial rather than based on personal relationships. Governance standardizes processes that otherwise would vary widely and result in inconsistent performance across projects.

Actually Achieving Benefits and ROI[7]

A governance process that requires project sponsors to report on actual benefits received can greatly increase those benefits. Even if projects are completed, they may not deliver value unless the sponsors and IT staff are supported and held accountable. For example, when adequate training does not occur or applications are down repeatedly, value is not received. Such risks need to be managed through monitoring and a defined risk-mitigation process. Resources need to be allocated and their availability ensured. IT governance must be interfaced to the project and portfolio management process.

ROI is very difficult to structure so that it is measurable. Business leaders from all departments own the projects and the results and may have changing priorities other than your ROI.

—Lynn H. Vogel, PhD, Vice President and
Chief Information Officer, The University of Texas
MD Anderson Cancer Center, Houston, TX

It is not typical for projects to come back to the governance committee to review whether the benefits of the project have been achieved. An exception is an organization where the CEO chairs the governance committee or, as in the case of Saint Luke's Health System (see the case study in Chapter 8), where the senior management committee also functions as the IT governance committee. The principal role of the governance committee is to determine if a project was implemented and whether it was on time and on budget. For example, a healthcare system may put in one central lab system with the expectation of capturing more referrals that are now going out to reference labs: "We're doing 50,000 tests now, but with the new central lab system, the number is going to increase to 70,000." Typically, the lab reports to a vice president of ancillary services, and that person keeps track of results and benefits: "Why are we doing 60,000 tests and not 70,000 after the project is finished?" It is not the role of IT to question whether benefits were received. The business sponsors and the executives to which they report have that role.

Aligning with Strategy

IT governance can be used to align IT spending with the strategies of the organization. Alignment can be achieved by formal processes, such as requiring that business plans submitted to the governance committee specify how the project will support one or more of the strategies of the organization. This is a requirement of the governance processes at both Saint Luke's Health System in Kansas City, MO (see Chapter 8) and Eastern Maine Healthcare Systems (EMHS) in Brewer (see Chapter 7).

Providing Input to the Capital Budgeting Process

IT governance can suggest the priorities for capital spending on IT and help the board and senior executives decide how much to allocate to IT in relation to other needs.

Managing Demand for IT

IT governance is needed because there is an almost infinite need for IT and finite resources available to the organization. Without governance, projects are accepted and many are never started. Those that are started may not be the most important for achieving the organization's strategies.

What IT Governance Covers

Effective IT governance addresses three questions:
1. What decisions must be made to ensure effective management and use of IT?
2. Who should make those decisions?
3. How will these decisions be made and monitored?[8]

> Fundamentally, IT governance is concerned about two things: IT's delivery of value to the business and mitigation of IT risks. The first is driven by strategic alignment of IT with the business. The second is driven by embedding accountability into the enterprise. Both need to be supported by adequate resources and measured to ensure that the results are obtained.

> This leads to the five main focus areas for IT governance, all driven by stakeholder value. Two of them are outcomes: value delivery and risk management. Three of them are drivers: strategic alignment, resource management (which overlays them all) and performance measurement.[9]

What Decisions Need to Be Made?

Weill and Ross believe that five interrelated decision types need to be addressed in governance:[10]
- **IT Principles**—Clarifying the business role of IT
- **IT Architecture**—Defining integration and standardization requirements
- **IT Infrastructure**—Determining shared and enabling services
- **Business Application Needs**—Specifying the business need for purchased or internally developed IT applications
- **IT Investment and Prioritization**—Choosing which initiatives to fund and how much to spend

Who provides input to these decisions and who makes them are important to identify in establishing a governance process.

Examples of IT principles that a hospital or health system might adopt are as follows:
1. Move from a department focus to an enterprise focus.
2. Create a balance between focusing on care delivery and research and education.
3. Become an IT early adopter to innovate in very high-value areas.
4. Utilize a cluster of core vendors with specialized applications.
5. Consider soft benefits with some return on investment (ROI) calculations.
6. Centralize planning, change control and system administration.

Strategic Alignment

IT projects are undertaken for many reasons, not all of them related to pursuing the strategy of an organization. Some are undertaken to meet the demands of influential stakeholders or regulatory agencies. Others are pursued to acquire cutting-edge technology for its own sake. IT governance seeks to focus on achieving value in relation to the strategy of an organization. For example, if clinical excellence in a medical specialty is considered highly important, then IT projects that help achieve that should be given high priority.

EMHS has defined six strategic pillars and the goals and objectives for them. The strategic pillars are people, quality, service, finance, growth and community.[11] Michelle Hood, EMHS's CEO, believes alignment is achieved not through the governance process, but by including IT as a component of strategic planning and the process of creating capital and operating budgets. "Projects are no longer seen as IT projects, but strategic projects. They are enabled by IT," said Hood (see the EMHS case study in Chapter 7).

Project Prioritization

The IT steering or governance committee needs to set transparent criteria for project prioritization. For example:
- Project aligned with business goals?
  - Strategic or operational priority?
  - Regulatory/maintenance requirement?
- Sufficient organizational commitment?
  - Problem defined and process examined?
  - Current process/system optimized?
  - Executive sponsor identified and accountable?
- Sufficient organizational capability?
  - Funding (capital, ongoing operational)?
  - Required prerequisites in place?
  - Mature solutions/products available?
  - Sufficient IT and user resources?
  - Sufficient operational impact?
  - Metrics/ROI identified?

Value Estimation and Delivery[12]

Value Delivery—Creating new value for the enterprise through IT, maintaining and increasing value derived from existing IT investments and eliminating IT initiatives and assets that are not creating sufficient value for the enterprise. The basic principles of IT value are delivery of fit-for-purpose services and solutions on time and within budget, and generating the financial and non-financial benefits that were intended. The value that IT delivers should be aligned directly with the values on which the business is focused and measured in a way that transparently shows the impacts and contribution of the IT-enabled investments in the value creation process of the enterprise.[13]

Risk Management

Risk Management—Addressing IT-related risks. IT risk is the business risk associated with the use, ownership, operation, involvement, influence and adoption of IT within an enterprise. IT risk consists of IT-related events that could potentially impact the business. While value delivery focuses on the creation of value, risk management focuses on the preservation of value.[14]

Risk management is a formal part of project management. Project management guidelines, such as the Project Management Body of Knowledge published by the Project Management Institute (www.pmi.org/), provide specific steps for identifying risk and creating a risk mitigation plan. This is a task assigned to project managers and a project management office, if one exists.

Resource Management

Resource Management—Ensuring that the right capabilities are in place to execute the strategic plan and sufficient, appropriate and effective resources are provided. Resource management ensures that an integrated, economical IT infrastructure is provided, new technology is introduced as required by the business and obsolete systems are updated or replaced. It recognizes the importance of people, in addition to hardware and software, and, therefore, focuses on providing training, promoting retention and ensuring competence of key IT personnel.[15]

Performance Measurement

Performance Measurement—Tracking the achievement of the objectives of the enterprise's IT-related services and solutions and compliance with specific external requirements. Without establishing and monitoring performance measures, it is unlikely that the previous focus areas will achieve their desired outcomes. The performance measurement area includes the creation of business-oriented IT scorecards, assessment and assurance activities and a focus on continual performance improvement. It provides a link back to the other focus areas by monitoring that the required direction is being followed and creates the opportunity to take timely corrective measures, if needed.[16]

Sentara Healthcare, located in southeastern Virginia, is comprised of eight hospitals, a 400-physician multi-specialty medical group, six outpatient campuses and 10 long-term-care facilities. The organization has realized significant financial, patient safety and quality benefits from the implementation of an EHR across its care delivery sites. Several of the many benefits include $9.4 million in savings due to length-of-stay reductions resulting from streamlined care processes; $3.9 million in savings from migrating to a paperless medical record environment; $4.4 million in increased outpatient revenue due to improved patient service and increased procedure volume; reductions in scheduling call center answer time (10 seconds from 71 seconds) and call abandonment rate (3% from 9%); reduction in medication order entry to administration time (4 minutes from 59 minutes); and the avoidance of over 88,000 potential medication errors due to bar code scanning alerts. Clear IT governance and executive and medical staff leadership accountability were critical in obtaining these outcomes and included:

- A rigorous EHR vendor selection, implementation planning and benefits identification process;
- An Executive Design Committee responsible for EHR design and implementation decisions (comprised of senior leaders across Sentara hospitals and physician practices);
- A Physician Advisory Group responsible for vendor selection, software design, EHR implementation and ongoing optimization (comprised of community physician leaders from Sentara's major inpatient and ambulatory specialties who were compensated for their time);
- A medical director at each hospital and physician practice that provided leadership and worked with the medical staff, hospital Physician IT Steering Committees and Medical Staff Officers Council to provide oversight;
- Developing and gaining commitment on how the EHR initiative would be instrumental in supporting a compelling and common vision of the future; and
- Mapping benefits to operational processes and holding process owners accountable for results by embedding benefits in operational leaders' performance goals and budgets.

Source: Aspen Advisors[17]

Governance Is Not Just Oversight

> One coach said, "We don't play not to lose. We play to win." Governance is not a defensive action. It's an opportunity to rethink the way an organization coordinates and controls its resources, the way it directs its energies toward positive, ethical, strategic purposes.[18]

Governance in some organizations refers only to oversight by committees and auditors looking for problems. As Meyer notes,[19] it is costly in terms of the time of the overseers and those who have to defend their decisions; it is ineffective because the committees cannot review every decision and catch every mistake; it can lead to the wrong answers because oversight rules must be simple and applied consistently regardless of the situation. Oversight is also disempowering because it separates authority from accountability.

> Oversight transfers some authority from those doing the job to those judging and controlling them. Whenever oversight separates accountability and authority, trouble can occur. In the worst case, those with authority but no accountability become tyrants; those with accountability but lacking concomitant authority become victims and scapegoats, set up to fail. The result is poor decisions by those with the power, ineffective performance by those who lack needed authorities, and an overall damper on entrepreneurship, creativity and initiative.[20]

Meyer believes that oversight is a mechanism of last resort. He calls the alternative "systemic governance," which induces "people to do the right thing in the first place."[21] Systemic governance addresses "all the processes that coordinate and control an organization's resources and actions,"[22] including:

- **Culture:** The behavioral patterns (habits and conventions) generally practiced within an organization.
- **Structure:** The definition of jobs and the reporting hierarchy (organization chart), as well as the processes that combine people into teams as work flows across organizational boundaries.
- **Internal Economy:** The budgeting, pricing (charge backs), priority-setting, project approval and tracking processes that determine how resources flow through an organization and to its clients.
- **Methods and Tools:** The procedures, methods, skills and tools that people use.
- **Metrics and Rewards:** The feedback loops that let people know how they are doing so they can adjust their behavior, and the incentives for improving performance.[23]

Meyer's definition of the areas that governance should address is consistent with Weill and Ross's idea that governance should "encourage desirable behavior in using IT."[24] But Meyer goes beyond their definition of governance as "specifying the decision rights and accountability framework." He recognizes that "organizations are still limited in the amount of change they can absorb at any one time."[25] Meyer suggests the alternatives of addressing only one problem (e.g., excessive costs) or a single system (e.g., structure) or of implementing changes to address all the problems, but in one system at a time (e.g., structure, then metrics and rewards).

Conclusion

The important point to remember is that governance is not just about enforcing rules and monitoring behavior, as in the oversight approach. Governance must also be designed to address more than just structure and must especially consider how governance will encourage desirable behavior. If the governance process is seen as negative ("where projects go to die"), it will not encourage positive behaviors. Business or clinical sponsors will be discouraged from bringing proposals or will seek ways to move projects forward by working outside the governance process. It is important for the governance committee to consider how it reviews proposals. Rather than just criticizing, it can adopt a consultative role by, for instance, explaining to a proposer how to make a project's benefits or ROI clearer. Rather than rejecting projects outright, it can assign priorities to proposals and let them go forward for further review by the finance committee of the board. The governance committee should encourage people to bring projects they see a need for.

We will consider structure in more detail in Chapter 3 and will further examine processes, workflows and project management in Chapter 4 and Chapter 5.

Chapter 2

Keys to Successful IT Governance

The literature on healthcare and corporate IT governance identifies keys, or critical success factors, for effective IT governance. Healthcare executives interviewed for this book have added their own judgments, which are quoted in this chapter. The keys to success include the careful definition of who is responsible and accountable for decisions. For example, IT staff should not be the primary sponsors of projects, so clinical and management sponsors must be involved from the beginning, as well as the people who will actually use the systems implemented.

The executives interviewed for this book also identified mistakes you can make in IT governance, including ignoring critics, especially physicians, rather than engaging them and even putting them on governance committees so they can understand the issues and processes better.

Critical Success Factors in IT Governance
Communicate
The CEO needs to communicate the governance process to the organization. A charter should be prepared and widely disseminated from the CEO. The CEO communicates that the process must be followed and that projects are not to be submitted to the CEO or the board directly. Deadlines for submission of proposals to the advisory committees and the governance committee are defined.

You need to be out there with the customer and not sitting in your office. You are going to have difficult times in governance and you need the personal relationships.
— Jim Burton, Senior Vice President and Chief Information Officer, East Jefferson General Hospital, Metairie, LA

Closing the feedback loop causes people to do things a different way.

You have to get back to them after they propose a project. If you don't get back to them, they will find another way to get the project done.
— Janice Kishner, Vice President and Chief Nursing Executive, East Jefferson General Hospital, Metairie, LA

Meet Regularly

The governance committee needs to meet regularly and follow the finance committee calendar for submission of proposals. Do not be afraid to cancel meetings when no decisions need to be made. Committee members will stop coming if they believe that they lack real authority and that meetings are just for updates or presentations. Meetings are for considering new projects, setting priorities and reviewing existing and completed projects.

Do Not Be Afraid to Rotate Members

Senior managers and clinicians do not have to serve on every committee for every term. Allow them to nominate others to the committee, but do not allow substitutions for individual meetings. Senior managers and clinicians must be able to say, however, that the person nominated speaks for them. For example, the medical director might appoint a medical department head to a committee. That person has to commit to serving for a specified term (e.g., a year). Members who cannot attend a meeting are not allowed to vote on that meeting's issues, nor are they allowed to send a substitute. Explaining the committee's tasks and processes to one-time attendees would waste too much time.

Do Not Allow Gaming

As stated earlier, the CEO needs to communicate that the process will be followed and that no IT project will be allowed to proceed unless it has gone through the governance process. Moreover, it should be impossible to skirt the governance process by breaking a project into pieces, each of which falls below the threshold for submission. To avoid this, the threshold for review can be set at a very low level (e.g., 80 hours of work for IT and $10,000).

Some project sponsors may also try to circumvent the governance process by understating their budgets. For example, they may include the cost of software but not the data conversion or hardware costs. To avoid this, the project managers in IT who review smaller projects need to carefully consider each proposal to identify needed components and a realistic budget. The facts of a proposal may be verified by speaking directly to vendors.

There's going to be conflict and the person at the top needs to be able to enforce the governance process. Governance is about trust. If you have people gaming the system and winning approval for their projects, the governance process loses all credibility.
— Jim Burton, Senior Vice President and Chief Information
Officer, East Jefferson General Hospital, Metairie, LA

Senior-level people need to tell people who have tried to go around the process that they are aware of what has happened and should remind them that the governance process must be followed. For example, if a project got to the governance committee without being reviewed by one of the subcommittees, a senior manager should find out how that happened and then tell the proposal's sponsor that such a shortcut must not happen again.

We need to use those moments for education.

—Janice Kishner, Vice President and Chief Nursing Executive,
East Jefferson General Hospital, Metairie, LA

Have an Expedited Process for Smaller Projects

The governance committee should establish an expedited review process for smaller projects. Doing so will reduce the concern that the governance process will cause significant delays. It will also help to trim the work load created by setting thresholds low enough to discourage gaming. When an expedited small-project process is in place, the governance committee will not feel they are wasting time looking at insignificant projects.

Recognize the Importance of Good Staff Work

Staff need to support the process by thoroughly reviewing the projects. IT staff and the governance and advisory committees need to define the questions to be answered (e.g., what is the project's return on investment?) to avoid repeatedly returning proposals for more information. If each proposal is expected to be accompanied by a completed form, then staff should ensure that each form is complete before it is sent to a committee. Minutes are important and should define all the actions that need to be taken after the meeting. The minutes need to be widely disseminated so that everybody knows what is being proposed and what has to be done.

Align What You Are Doing with the Organization and Its Culture

You want to make sure your process supports your organization's overall goals and strategic plan. You have to include the organization's goals and strategies in the process, for example, in the business plan.

You can be out in front too far. I've tried to be out in front in developing the process, for example, in requiring business plans. I try to listen to their feedback. We've decentralized some of the decision-making but now are in the process of moving toward greater centralization. The incentive program for Meaningful Use has greatly increased the degree to which we work together.

—Cathy Bruno, Chief Information Officer,
Eastern Maine Healthcare Systems, Brewer, ME

Recognize That IT Should Not Own the Process and Make the Decisions

The goal is both a process and outcome. The process should not be CIO dependent. The CIO should lay out the facts and give an opinion, but not make a decision. The business sponsor has to drive the decision.

— Jim Burton, Senior Vice President and Chief Information
Officer, East Jefferson General Hospital, Metairie, LA

Keep It Simple and Transparent

Effective governance is simple and transparent. The governance process unambiguously defines the responsibility or objective for a specific person or group. How the process works is clear to those who are affected by or want to challenge governance decisions.

Everyone should know how the process operates and senior managers communicate that. For example, the CMIO (chief medical information officer) can be viewed as a marketing person for IT, explaining decisions physician to physician.
—Deborah Gash, Vice President and Chief Information Officer,
Saint Luke's Health System, Kansas City, MO

Be really clear and communicate a lot. Build relationships and make sure they know what you're doing and what your decision processes are. There shouldn't be any surprises.
—Cathy Bruno, Chief Information Officer,
Eastern Maine Healthcare Systems, Brewer, ME

Physicians want to know how decisions are made. They want some processes embedded in policy. Physicians and nurses can go online and raise an issue about the EMR and that issue will be tracked until it's resolved. Others will go to the CMIO and CMO (chief medical officer) and raise the concern directly.
—Erik Steele, Chief Medical Officer,
Eastern Maine Healthcare Systems, Brewer, ME

Have a clear process for presenting projects to the governance committee. Determine the criteria you should use to determine if a project should go forward. Give the individual entities of the system some guidance on the amount of work they should be pushing up to the governance committee. The governance committee should have an overall vision of how the pieces are going to fit together and advise the individual entities on what they're supposed to do.
—Eric Hartz, Chief Medical Information Officer,
Eastern Maine Medical Center, Bangor, ME

A process that does not define responsibilities and objectives allows sponsors to argue later that someone else was accountable. Processes that are complex and ambiguous encourage clinicians and managers to go around them. For example, proposal sponsors can break projects into pieces that individually cost less than the threshold that requires submission to the governance process. Sponsors will also try to expedite a project by asking for approval from a senior executive rather than going through the governance process, arguing that the project is an exception.

Make the process very transparent. Keep track of meeting notes, decisions, ownership and communicate widely. Be as inclusive as possible. Strong representation from every department is needed. The process must be driven by the operational owners.
—David L. Miller, Vice Chancellor and Chief Information Officer,
University of Arkansas for Medical Sciences, Little Rock, AR

Create a Level of Trust and Credibility

Deliver what you promised. People begin to realize that if they are involved in the governance process, they're going to get results.

—Jim Burton, Senior Vice President and Chief Information
Officer, East Jefferson General Hospital, Metairie, LA

You have to have a plausible approach to governance and how you're organized. It has to be well communicated and understood. You have to have the credibility so that governance is believed and trusted. There has to be some confidence that during the governance process, when decisions are made or directions are taken, it will go well.

—Eric Yablonka, Vice President and Chief Information Officer,
University of Chicago Medical Center, Chicago, IL

Prepare the Organization for the Governance Process

. . . the best governance design in the world, mandated by the highest levels in the organization and championed by a senior management advocate, will not succeed if the participants are not ready for the change or do not participate in the design process.[26]

Most managers and clinicians will not read or pay attention to the governance process until they have a project for which it is required. It is still important to talk with a wide group of managers and clinicians. In some hospitals, the need will be obvious to everyone because, for example, major projects are failing and there are severe cost overruns.

Factors That Contribute to Organizational Readiness. Many factors can contribute to predisposed organizational readiness for enhanced IT governance:

- A significant, spectacular and/or costly IT failure attributed to lack of communication, direction or controls.
- An unfavorable audit or regulatory finding concerning IT governance or IT controls.
- An acquisition, merger or other significant change in direction, visibility or dependence of the organization on IT.
- Environmental factors that can cause, or have caused, the organization to be "change ready," such as a return to growth after downsizing or an economic recession.[27]

Socialize the Need

A frequent error committed here is to just announce the need. This top-down approach invariably leads to resistance and failure in all but the most hierarchical, authoritarian-type organizations. Instead, meetings, work groups and planning sessions in which the symptoms are discussed and solutions sought must precede design efforts for most organizations. This sensitizes the organization to the need, gains commitment and creates organizational readiness.[28]

Actively Design Governance

Many enterprises have created disparate IT governance mechanisms. These uncoordinated mechanism "silos" result from governance by default—introducing mechanisms one at a time to address a particular need (for example, architecture problems or overspending or duplication). Patching up problems as they arise is a defensive tactic that limits opportunities for strategic impact from IT. Instead, management should actively design IT governance around the enterprise's objectives and performance goals. . . . One goal of any governance redesign should be to assess, improve and then consolidate the number of mechanisms. Early in the learning cycle, mechanisms may involve large numbers of managers. Typically, as senior managers better understand IT value and the role of IT, a smaller set of managers can represent enterprise needs.[29]

Multiple IT governance mechanisms are sometimes developed as a result of history. A governance committee may be created after a committee has been developed to oversee the implementation of an EHR system. The latter committee is chaired by the CMO or CMIO, while the governance committee is chaired by the CIO. Because of the size and expense of implementing an EHR system, it may seem like a good idea to create a governance body with broader representation than the IT governance committee. However, the two groups would work on the same issues, resulting in some confusion and inefficiencies. Who should consider infrastructure development, e.g., network development and storage? A solution is to create a single decision-making structure by making the EHR committee a subcommittee of the IT governance committee.

Involve Executives in the Governance Process

Executive involvement is critically important for holding the clinical and business sponsors, as well as IT leaders, accountable for project success. Executive involvement is also vital for ensuring that resources are actually available until projects are completed. Executives must also ensure adherence to the governance process so that the benefits of governance are received.

The personal investment of the Chief Medical Officer in the process is key. The CMO has to understand how decisions are made. CMOs have to make sure that issues get tracked and resolved. The loop has to be closed back to the initiating physician. The CMIO and the CMO have to be partners. The CMO needs to be involved in key discussions to make sure that the physician perspective is represented. You have to make sure the physician's voice is effective in decision-making.

—Erik Steele, Chief Medical Officer,
Eastern Maine Healthcare Systems, Brewer, ME

Executive and Board Roles and Responsibilities.[30] While executive and board involvement is always cited as important in IT governance, translating that into specific roles and responsibilities is not easy or obvious. Top-level executives and board members have many other issues to deal with. The task is to define roles and responsibilities that result in the effective allocation of resources and successful projects. For example, the CIO usually chairs the governance committee. The CIO's staff prepares the proposal that goes forward to the finance committee after the governance committee's approval. Senior executives should be project sponsors monitoring the achievement of major project milestones (with the assistance of project managers). Roles and responsibilities are usually defined by creating a series of committees with the necessary authority.

Engage Clinical and Management Leadership

A successful governance process includes thoughtful engagement by leaders and others in your organization and active participation by stakeholders. That is success. The CIO's role is not necessarily to deliver on what we promise. We need to have the organization own IT and decide the priorities. We should get significant input. Without that, if the organization doesn't own IT, they don't own the spend and they won't own the outcomes. If they don't own outcomes and the outcomes are not achieved, it's the CIO's fault. It's a team sport, not an individual sport. Success involves the organization owning IT.
—Eric Yablonka, Vice President and Chief Information Officer, University of Chicago Medical Center, Chicago, IL

The leaders of the organization need to be involved not only in planning but also in executing.

We have executive sponsors for all of our projects. They do a lot of the reporting to the board and senior leadership. It has to be someone who is on the management committee. They can designate a project sponsor from the relevant department.
—Deborah Gash, Vice President and Chief Information Officer, Saint Luke's Health System, Kansas City, MO

It is much easier to get senior management and clinical leaders to engage in the process and contribute when they know decisions are going to be made and systems actually implemented. If meetings are held to provide information only, commitment and attendance can drop off.

When you have money to allocate, you can have bottom up governance processes; but when money is scarce, governance proceeds from the top down.
—Lynn H. Vogel, PhD, Vice President and Chief Information Officer, The University of Texas MD Anderson Cancer Center, Houston, TX

Engage Physicians and Nurses

Physicians and chief nursing officers must have input into the prioritization and configuration of applications.

Physicians need to feel they are just as important as the business side. If there are templates, physicians need to know what they are, agree that they will be functional, and have significant input on configuration.

—George Pagels, Chief Medical Officer, Saint Luke's
Health System and Chief Executive Officer,
Saint Luke's East, Kansas City, MO

Nurses have to trust that I will be carrying their message forward. They have to trust the governance structure. It is important to recognize that there are going to be mistakes and be willing to admit them to users.

—Gloria Solis, Chief Nursing Officer, Saint Luke's East,
Saint Luke's Health System, Kansas City, MO

Assign Ownership and Accountability for IT Governance

Our recommendation is that the board or CEO hold the CIO accountable for IT governance performance with some clear measures of success. Most CIOs will then create a group of senior business and IT managers to help design and implement IT governance. The action of the board or CEO to appoint and announce the CIO as accountable for IT governance performance is an essential first step in raising the stakes for IT governance. Without that action, some CIOs cannot engage their senior management colleagues in IT governance. Alternatively, the board or CEO may identify a group to be accountable for IT governance performance. This group will then often designate the CIO to design and implement IT governance.[31]

Provide the Right Incentives

. . . a common problem we encountered in studying IT governance was a misalignment of incentive and reward systems with the behaviors the IT governance arrangements were designed to encourage. . . . IT governance is less effective when incentive and reward systems are not aligned with organizational goals. . . . Avoiding financial disincentives to desirable behavior is as important as offering financial incentives. . . . It is hard to overestimate the importance of aligning incentive and reward systems to governance arrangements. If well-designed IT governance is not as effective as expected, the first place to look is incentives.[32]

The IT governance process should reward project sponsors who adhere to the rules by providing them with the funds and support for implementation through a clearly defined, efficient process. If the process instead delays projects or requires effort that prevents other work from being done, an incentive is created for potential project sponsors to avoid the process. If those who are successful in avoiding the governance process are seen as being rewarded by earlier implementation and improved performance, the governance process is undermined. For example, a project sponsor wants approval of an upgrade to a picture archiving and communication system that would allow access to images across multiple facilities. In response, the department chair makes a plea directly to the CEO and board and receives funding for the project. When the department receives praise from physicians for the improved access, other potential project sponsors can see incentives and rewards for bypassing the governance process.

A hospital had an Operating Room (OR) system that provided the reports it needed but did not connect to the other systems in the hospital. A physician looking at a patient's medical record could see all services except those in the OR. Clinicians had created 200 reports that would have to be rewritten if the OR module in the hospital's EHR system was adopted. To provide incentive, the CIO offered to engage a consultant to write the reports and to add an anesthesia module not in the current system.

The governance process should reward those who comply with it and propose or accept changes that benefit the organization. The CEO should communicate that projects will not be approved without moving through the governance process.

Assess if the Governance Process Is Effective
In Chapter 1, we noted that Weill and Ross define IT governance as "specifying the decision rights and accountability framework to encourage desirable behavior in IT usage." They go on to say that "governance performance must then be how well the governance arrangements encouraged desirable behaviors and ultimately how well the firm achieved its desired performance goals."[33]

Symptoms of Ineffective Governance. Weill and Ross identify the following symptoms of ineffective governance:
1. **Senior Management Senses Low Value from IT Investments.** Senior managers typically react in one of several ways to this concern. Some managers dive in to learn more about IT, making more IT decisions personally and centralizing control. Others abdicate responsibility to colleagues such as managers in the IT unit because they are unsure how to act or don't think it's important. Still other senior managers engage consultants or make new hires to "fix the problem." Rather than starting with increasing control, abdication, or bringing in new people, first look at IT governance. Perhaps the wrong people are making IT decisions or the people making those decisions need management education. Good governance will produce metrics supporting or contradicting management's gut feeling. If everyone on the senior management team cannot point to a record of how recent IT investments have been performing, governance is a problem.[34]
2. **IT Is Often a Barrier to Implementing New Strategies.** Instead of acting as a strategic enabler, does IT often act as a barrier? If IT limits the ability to respond to new market opportunities, the IT infrastructure may be broken.[35]
3. **The Mechanisms to Make IT Decisions Are Slow or Contradictory.** Effective governance comes from a set of well-designed and well-executed mechanisms that reinforce desirable behavior. Are different mechanisms sending contradictory messages to executives?. . . Just as troubling are mechanisms that obstruct rather than

support project implementations. . . . If the exception process is not fast and predictable, individuals will be motivated to act outside the system. If renegade exceptions are in evidence, governance is a problem.[36]

4. **Senior Management Cannot Explain IT Governance.** We know from our research that the more managers in leadership positions there are who can accurately describe IT governance, the better the governance performance. . . . In particular, senior managers know what decisions IT makes and what decisions they must make. . . . If fewer than 50 percent of managers in leadership positions can accurately describe IT governance, and the number is not increasing every month, governance is a problem.[37]

5. **IT Projects Often Run Late and Over Budget.** A number of studies over the last ten years in several countries found that the percentage of IT projects completed on time and on budget is typically less than half. Effective IT governance should provide consistency in project management and program design. Project management should ensure allocation of dedicated resources, a disciplined sequence of stages, and formal project tracking. Good project management leads to predictable project delivery. If 90 percent of projects are not delivered on time and on budget, governance is a problem.[38]

6. **Senior Management Sees Outsourcing as a Quick Fix to IT Problems.** Selective outsourcing of IT capability can be a very effective management strategy. . . . However, some outsourcing decisions result from frustration with IT. Concerned about IT costs or lack of value, managers turn to outsourcing as a quick fix to control the problem. . . . To be effective, outsourcing should result from a decision that particular competencies or services are better provided externally. . . . Outsourcing as a quick fix motivated by frustration with IT outcomes suggests that governance is a problem.[39]

7. **Governance Changes Frequently.** Management is what decisions are made. Management decisions typically change as strategies change. Governance is who makes the decisions, and thus changes less often than strategy. Changing governance every time you change strategy should not be necessary as many of the governance mechanisms, such as committees and budgets, are independent of strategy. Governance should change only when a change in strategy prompts a change in desirable behaviors. For example, a shift from a customer intimacy to a product leadership discipline would signal a change in how much business unit collaboration is valued. This more radical shift in strategy—a change in strategic intent—would be likely to drive changes in governance. Frequent changes in IT governance almost guarantee ineffective IT use. Unable to comprehend or keep up with the changes, managers are likely to completely ignore governance.[40]

Another symptom is bypassing of the governance process. If there are other ways to get projects approved, e.g., a direct appeal to the CEO or CFO, then the governance process is not going to be able to assure that projects are successful, are aligned with organizational priorities and are completed on time and within budget.

The governance process should also be identifying important needs, such as infrastructure upgrades and the physicians' need for mobile and remote access. There should not be an imbalance of the IT capabilities and resources between the business and clinical functions of the organization. Are clinicians provided with an EHR system while finance has difficulty producing accurate bills?

Mistakes and Lessons Learned
Providing Too Much Information
Michelle Hood, President and CEO of Eastern Maine Healthcare Systems (EMHS), believes it is a mistake to provide too much detailed information to people involved in governance. Information needs to be filtered. Providing too much information puts them in the role of management. "It's a fine line," Hood says. "They should be involved in issues like Meaningful Use and the use of informatics to support new care delivery systems."

Assuming People Understand
You shouldn't operate in a vacuum and assume that people understand what the plan is and the implications of that plan.
—Eric Yablonka, Vice President and Chief Information Officer,
University of Chicago Medical Center, Chicago, IL

Not Engaging the Critics
Remember that the people who don't agree with you are not your enemy. Bring the people who are the loudest critics into the process.
—Christopher Barrilleaux, Chief Medical Information Officer,
East Jefferson General Hospital, Metairie, LA

Engage naysayers in the process. People who are critics can be very helpful.
—Eric Yablonka, Vice President and Chief Information Officer,
University of Chicago Medical Center, Chicago, IL

Do not take criticism personally. Cathy Bruno, CIO at EMHS, believes you should not express frustration and take criticism personally. "You need to engage your constituents in a positive way," Bruno says.

Having an Unclear Process for IT Funding or Poor Staff Support
Erik Steele, CMO at EMHS, believes that having an unclear process in defining how much money IT gets is a mistake. "If there is a lot of variability so that IT gets less money during the year, the IT governance process is degraded. The confidence of the IT governance members is degraded," Steele says. He believes that inadequate staff support for IT governance is also a mistake. "Good background information is needed well in advance. Good minutes that are action oriented are needed to provide credibility," he adds.

Not Prioritizing Against Objective Criteria

Good prioritization is comparing every application to every other application according to the criteria. If the criterion is patient safety, then every application needs to be compared on that. That's hard work, but if you do that you wind up with something that has face validity. It's acceptable to everyone.

—George Pagels, Chief Medical Officer, Saint Luke's
Health System and Chief Executive Officer of
Saint Luke's East, Lees Summit, MO

Other Mistakes to Avoid

Jim Burton, Senior Vice President and CIO of East Jefferson General Hospital (EJGH), Metairie, Louisiana, believes there are three major mistakes to avoid:

- **Compromising on what's right to make pressure go away.** This dilutes the influence of the CIO. When the CIO is willing to deviate from the process, credibility is lost.
- **Not starting the governance process when you first arrive.** Once the spigot of projects has been opened, it is difficult to turn it off. You need to slow down the evaluation process while the governance process develops.
- **Allowing a siloed process that separates physicians, nurses and managers.** When Burton arrived at EJGH there were too many committees. The process was siloed. Physicians and nurses had separate committees and never met together. There is now a weekly meeting where the CMIO, the CNO, the medical director and the CIO meet to discuss changes related to clinical projects.

Judy Brown, CFO of EJGH, believes there are two mistakes to avoid:

- **Make sure that the IT department does not prioritize projects before they enter the governance process.** Doing so could push projects down that should have a higher priority.
- **Do not let departments, including IT, go around the process.** Try to get IT involved from the beginning. This helps avoid disappointment because people often do not understand the implications of their project in terms of resources and impact on other projects.

Chapter 3

Committee Structure

A number of considerations enter into determining committee structure. Authority, time and expertise are important factors. One common governance structure is a hierarchy of committees, where the most important is an IT governance or steering committee consisting of the most senior managers and clinicians, including the chief executive officer (CEO), chief operating officer (COO), chief financial officer (CFO) and chief information officer (CIO). This committee prioritizes projects and holds others accountable for project success. Since the members lack specific expertise in the clinical or business areas affected, advisory committees are needed. For example, a clinical systems committee would advise on all proposed clinical IT projects. That committee, however, would not have the time to oversee the implementation of more than a few projects. Therefore, a committee is needed for each major project that includes the executive sponsor, the clinical or business sponsor most affected and IT staff.

Who will agree to participate and will they commit to the process? You need to identify senior managers and clinicians who are willing to dedicate the time, do not see committee membership as a ceremonial position and have the best interests of the whole institution in mind.

Stakeholders in IT Governance
Physicians
The role, authority and influence of physicians needs to be considered in determining a committee structure. Many physicians are interested in attending a meeting where a project of personal importance is being discussed, but participants in the governance process need to commit to working on a whole range of projects. Multiple perspectives are needed to make good decisions. If a physician is believed to be an essential member of a committee, the CEO may have to be involved and compensation may need to be offered. Whether and how much physicians are compensated depends on the organization's culture. Some hospitals will pay non-employee physicians an annual stipend, while others will offer per-hour compensation. EMHS pays physicians who are not employed by EMHS or its members on a per-hour basis. If physicians are being paid for another role, such as medical director, committee time is included in the duties they are compensated for. Physicians who are employed by EMHS get dedicated time and are not penalized if they are paid partly on productivity (see the EMHS case study in Chapter 7).

Governance or Steering Committee

The governance or steering committee governs all IT projects and should be chaired by the CIO. The committee should include the CFO or another senior finance person. Also needed is a top-level general management person, preferably the COO. Senior nursing leadership should also be on the committee, as well as a building services executive. Senior medical staff who are employed in administration and paid by the institution should also be included, as well as independent physicians who admit patients.

Advisory Committees

Advisory committees often originate projects as well as review those that are submitted to them by representatives from the various departments. The advisory committees also provide an easily identified starting point for expressing concerns about existing systems. A system installed two years ago may not be functioning well and this structure gives staff somewhere to present the issues. All committees should have a senior IT staff member. Typically, IT staff members do not have a role in project management but can help validate and interpret the technology.

Healthcare organizations differ in the roles they give to advisory committees in the governance process.

Saint Luke's Health System, Kansas City, Missouri, does not have an IT governance committee. The organization's management committee carries out the functions of IT governance. Deborah Gash, Saint Luke's CIO, notes, "We have a flat organization and the people who run the management committee would typically also be on the IT steering committee. The management committee has delegated some of the decision-making about what's critical to the organization to prioritization groups. These committees, therefore, perform one of the functions of a steering committee." Saint Luke's has both a clinical applications prioritization group and a business systems prioritization group. As the names suggest, they prioritize projects in their areas (see Chapter 8).

The IS governance committee at EMHS has only one advisory group. The IS directors group provides input on policies and anything that is taken to the IS governance committee. The directors group provides a forum for the IS directors from each facility to discuss common issues, such as the different ways that facilities are handling personal portable devices. They also generate project requests but are not asked to prioritize projects. There are other advisory groups for major projects, such as Meaningful Use, but they do not report to the IS governance committee (see Chapter 7).

Board of Directors

A finance committee of the board of directors usually approves budgets and projects. In smaller organizations there may be at best one or two people on the board who understand IT projects and so the board relies heavily on the IT governance committee. In larger organizations, there may be board members who have in-depth IT knowledge and experience and have more independent views.

The Role of the CEO

Organizations differ in their extent of CEO involvement in IT governance. David Miller, Vice Chancellor and Chief Information Officer, University of Arkansas for Medical Sciences, believes the CEO should always be a member of the governance committee, even if participation is sporadic. The CEO of EMHS chairs the IS governance committee (see the case study in Chapter 7). EJGH has an information management steering committee (IMSC) that is chaired by the CIO but has the CEO as its executive sponsor (see the case study in Chapter 6).

Some CEOs choose to be involved only when projects are large, expensive or controversial. Other CEOs review proposals when they come to the finance committee on which they sit. CEOs may choose to attend all meetings of the governance committee when there has been a history of significant problems, such as failed projects or financial losses. The large sums of money being spent to obtain stimulus funds by meeting Meaningful Use requirements, to meet Health Insurance Portability and Accountability Act (HIPAA) 5010 requirements, to convert to ICD-10 and to meet accountable care organization requirements are increasing the involvement of CEOs in IT governance.

Considerations in Determining Structure
Number of Committees

Complexity may increase the need for additional committees. Academic medical centers may feel the need to add committees to involve stakeholders and manage the many entities they control.

We are increasing the number of committees so they are more focused. For example, we have one group just focusing on revenue cycle issues. We added an EHR advisory committee and project-specific committees such as ambulatory implementation and anesthesia implementation.

— Eric Yablonka, Vice President and Chief Information Officer,
University of Chicago Medical Center, Chicago, IL

On the other hand, smaller organizations may feel that a simple structure works best. Jim Burton, EJGH's Senior Vice President and CIO, believes that EJGH is not big enough to require committees for each clinical area, for example, ambulatory care.

Major projects can create exceptions to a policy of not creating multiple advisory committees. This includes the implementation of an EMR system and meeting Meaningful Use requirements to obtain federal stimulus funds. While Eastern Maine Medical Center (EMMC) has only one advisory committee reporting directly to the IS governance committee, a separate structure with multiple committees was established for meeting Meaningful Use requirements (see Chapter 7).

Avoiding Meeting Fatigue

Another consideration is the need to avoid the meeting fatigue that can arise when multiple committees have overlapping membership. Kraatz, Lyons and Tomkinson comment on how this problem arose during the implementation of an ambulatory EMR system for Continuum Health Partners in New York:

> Continuum's first proposed structure, while it looked good on paper, created "meeting fatigue." Too many committees with too many overlapping team members created an impossible scheduling task for the project and its team members. After about three months of further discussion and repurposing the committees, a more efficient and streamlined structure was put into place that had each of the teams perform a few more functions than initially designed, but seemed to be a better fit and use of the limited resources. . . . A lesson learned is to start with less committees and teams and let it naturally transform throughout the implementation, rather than trying to create the perfect structure in the early stages.[41]

For example, it would be reasonable to put a physician leader on all three levels of committees—governance, clinical advisory and clinical project implementation. Yet putting the same person on committees at all three levels may be less effective because of the time commitment required. Dealing with meeting fatigue requires careful consideration of the need for multiple committees and how much overlap there should be in membership.

You need to spread out the responsibility and rotate people.
—David L. Miller, Vice Chancellor and Chief Information Officer,
University of Arkansas for Medical Sciences, Little Rock, AR

Rather than reducing the number of committees, consider involving more individuals. Responsibility can be diffused by engaging, for example, any physician who is willing to commit time. No one person needs to be at all the meetings. If the CEO needs to be on a number of committees, the CEO could be appointed to them all but asked to attend only the meetings where the CEO's participation is essential. The same is true for the CMIO. If the CEO or CMIO prefer not to serve on a committee, they can suggest a replacement, but that person would need to commit to serving the full term without substitution.

Conflicting Committee Roles

Meyer identifies three roles that could be carried out by a single committee or separate committees:

- A **Purser** (someone who focuses on financial constraints) representing customers and deciding priorities, such as which products and services to buy with the limited resources that are available.
- A **Focus Group** providing input from the customers' viewpoint on key decisions.

- An **Internal Board of Directors** that helps the organization plan its strategies and make key decisions.

Meyer believes that committees that adopt all three roles create conflicts of interest for the organizational representatives on the committee. For example:

> **Scenario 1: Board of Directors and Purser.** In its role as an internal Board of Directors, the committee's job is to help the organization succeed. But in its role as Purser, the typical committee member is a demanding customer who wants more for less. The typical committee with this role mixture favors its Purser role and demands that the organization cut back on reinvestments in its capabilities (e.g., product research, training, time for innovation), diverting time to customers' immediate needs. This role conflict results in an organization that finds itself "eating its seed corn." Lacking the resources for sustenance functions, its IS skills, products, and infrastructure become obsolete.
>
> **Scenario 2: Focus Group and Purser.** In its role as a Focus Group, the committee provides input when asked on specific planning decisions but has no real decision power. But in its role as Purser, the committee has the power to decide which projects will be approved. When asked for input on a strategic direction (as a Focus Group), the committee may feel it has the power to veto the idea (as a Purser) in order to retain the resources for current client projects. This role conflict leads to short-term thinking.[42]

You could argue that an IT governance or steering committee composed of the most senior executives would not face the conflict in adopting both the internal Board of Directors and the Purser roles. Balancing strategy and resource constraints is their job. When a governance committee of less senior managers and clinicians is given both roles, however, Meyer would argue that the conflict exists. When the governance committee is also given the Focus Group role, a conflict can also arise. Can the members provide objective comments on a proposal when they know they face the job of evaluating it in relation to organizational strategy and resource constraints? Shouldn't the proposal be examined first, e.g., for potential benefits and staff acceptance, by an advisory committee composed of individuals who know the service or department making the proposal?

A solution is to carefully consider the type of decision that needs to be made and provide a specific charge to an advisory committee. The role of the advisory committees is usually to review proposals, determine the return on investment and what the users want, and present the priorities to the governance committee. This gives the advisory committees the Focus Group role and part of the Purser role. The governance committee is left with the Board of Directors role and the Purser role but is not asked to determine the desirability of the product from the user perspective.

Sometimes the Purser role can be removed from the advisory committee because the governance committee has determined that a product has to be purchased. The question is which is the best product? Even if it is widely known that one product is more expensive than another, the governance committee may want a judgment about the differences between the products and may reserve for itself the decision on which one is purchased based on other considerations, for example, whether a particular unit in the organization has a greater need for one product as opposed to another. Other times, the advisory committee may be asked to determine if there is a return on investment after a proposal has been submitted, a part of the Purser role.

So, a hospital that has a preferred-vendor strategy may want an advisory committee to compare its vendor's module to another vendor's product to determine what would be given up by accepting the vendor's module.

Saint Luke's Health System has prioritization committees for clinical and business services. They review projects and prioritize them. The CIO and her staff try to de-emphasize financial return on investment and how difficult the project will be for IT to implement when they ask the committee to prioritize a project. They want them to focus on the value of the project. The group has the financial numbers, but the discussion tends to be about value. Using Meyer's terms, the CIO wants the advisory committees to adopt the Focus Group and Board of Directors roles, but not the Purser role. She does not want projects rejected or given a lower priority because of cost. The management committee (which functions as the IT governance committee) is expected to adopt the Purser and Board of Directors roles.

The membership of committees that adopt all three roles is hard to determine. While IT staff are needed in the Board of Directors role, they may not be appropriate in the Purser role, which would require them to help decide which IT projects will be funded. The Focus Group role should be taken by customers of potential projects.

Meyer argues that a "single IS steering committee given multiple roles is unlikely to be effective, and may very well become a source of confusion and frustration for all involved."[43] He believes that typically the most valuable role for an IS governance committee is that of Purser and that if there is a need for an internal Board of Directors, that role should be assigned to a separate committee. Focus groups can be convened as needed.

However, our earlier discussion of meeting fatigue suggests a dilemma. Multiple committees with clear, nonconflicting roles can result in the same individuals spending a lot of time in meetings. The CFO, who is needed on a committee devoted to making financial decisions, also needs to be involved in a committee developing strategy. Also, can funding decisions be made without careful consideration of strategy? For such reasons, as we noted at the beginning of this chapter, a single governance or steering committee may be needed. But if that is the option chosen, executives need to consider the conflicts described by Meyer and create additional advisory committees as needed.

Examples of Committees and Their Roles, Membership and Functions[44]
Role of the IT Governance Committee

Kenneth G. Rau believes that the IT governance committee, or council, receives its authority explicitly or implicitly from the board of directors and assumes responsibility across all business functions for

- Policy setting
- Control (budget approval, project authorization, performance appraisal)
- Performance measurement and reporting

> The council's assumption and effective execution of these three roles is seldom manifest from its inception. Rather, each role evolves over time with learning and maturation of the council. . . . At the time of initiation of the IT governance council [Stage 1] . . . learning needs are at their highest and none of the three roles is well differentiated or performed. Monitoring of projects, budgets, and occasionally operating statistics is often a role that evolves first. By Stage 2, the role of policy setting evolves furthest, most often due to the council's instigation, approval, and oversight of an IT strategy and plan. In Stage 3, budgetary and project controls are established, and finally the IT governance council identifies and sees to the establishment of appropriate key performance indicators and reporting, often directing and relying on an IT project office to perform this function. In Stage 4, all three roles are mature.[45]

At EJGH, the information management steering committee (IMSC) is chaired by the CIO but with the CEO as the executive sponsor (see Chapter 6). Members include the CFO, CMIO, medical director, chief nursing executive, vice president of marketing, vice president of business development and vice president outpatient services. According to the IT governance policy and procedures, the IMSC is a decision-making body composed of senior management team members, responsible for defining and providing guidance in the development, funding and support of the organization's corporate information management policy framework. The committee defines the information management framework via an Information Management Strategic Plan, as shown in Chapter 6. The committee monitors progress made against the plan through the use of various management reporting tools.

The IMSC is, therefore, charged with the three functions defined by Rau. Jim Burton, EJGH's CIO, has been particularly interested in developing a mature project management office to pursue the third stage described by Rau.

Saint Luke's Health System has adopted a very different structure (see Chapter 8). Saint Luke's management committee also serves as the senior governance body for IT. The members of the management committee are the system's CEO, CFO, CMO, CNO and CIO. Also included are the CEOs of each Saint Luke's Health System facility and the vice presidents of human resources, risk management and compliance, marketing, business development and public affairs. Deborah Gash, Saint Luke's CIO, explains, "We have a flat organization and the people who run the management committee would typically also be on the IT steering committee." As described earlier, the management committee has delegated some of the decision making about what is critical to the organization to prioritization groups. Those committees, therefore, perform one of the functions of a governance committee. The management committee performs all three functions described by Rau but relies on experts in specific areas to evaluate both needs and applications.

EMHS illustrates another alternative. An IS governance committee was created that is chaired by the CEO. The IS governance committee is appointed by the leadership council, which includes the senior managers of EMHS and the CEOs of member organizations. The members of the IS governance committee have no fixed terms. Four of the CEOs of member facilities are currently on the IS governance committee, and there is no defined rotation among the CEOs in the system. Other members of the IS governance committee are the EMHS CMO, CIO, CFO and vice president for continuum of care, as well as two hospital nurses and a CMIO. As described earlier, the governance committee has only one advisory committee reporting directly to it, the IS directors group, which is not asked to evaluate or prioritize projects. Assessment of the costs of a project is done internally by IS staff and presented to the governance committee for review. Prioritization of projects is done by IS for infrastructure needed system-wide and by individual facilities for their own needs. Of the three functions described by Rau, the governance committee is most involved in setting policy. It shares the functions of control and performance measurement with member facilities and IS staff.

Role of Advisory Committees

Proposals for IT projects arrive over the course of the year. The advisory committees, which focus on assigned clinical or business areas, triage proposals and advise on which to pursue and when. They can also define interim solutions for multiyear projects. For example, replacement of a major system such as financial management might occur over several years.

Proposals that involve regulatory compliance, patient safety or a mandated vendor upgrade may not go to an advisory committee. Some are brought directly to a steering committee member. After the decision is made to proceed, some of those proposals may be sent down to an advisory committee for specialized help, such as advice on selecting a specific product. However, not all proposals are sent back down to an advisory committee.

Proposals are rarely rejected by an advisory committee. The advisory committee may give a proposal low priority, but more often the question is when to proceed or whether there is an alternative way to get the same benefit.

> **Governance at Beth Israel Deaconess Medical Center in Boston**
> The role of the overall IT governance committee at Beth Israel
> Deaconess Medical Center in Boston includes:
> - Communicating about prioritization and resource decisions.
> - Articulating, prioritizing and monitoring the overall vision for IT at
>   the medical center.
> - Achieving the right balance between built and bought systems,
>   including adequate staffing for maintenance to ensure high cus-
>   tomer satisfaction.
>
> *Source: John Halamka, CIO*[46]

A separate advisory committee should not be created for each department. In order to prioritize projects, the needs of multiple departments have to be weighed. When competing demands for clinical IT arise, it is the job of the clinical IT advisory committee to determine the priorities for spending in a particular year.

In a system of multiple hospitals, the leaders of a particular department may need to meet to discuss issues. For example, all the leaders of the hospitals' radiology departments may need to meet, but rarely do they need to meet just to discuss IT. When an IT issue arises, whether they meet or not, the departments can send a proposal to a clinical IT systems committee. For example, if the leadership of the hospital system's radiology departments decide that there is a need to consolidate and standardize their picture archiving and communication systems, they can send a proposal to the clinical systems advisory committee. If that committee needs further information, they can ask the departments for specialized help. The job of the advisory committee is to prioritize the needs of a variety of departments. Having multiple department-specific advisory committees would push more trade-off decisions to the governance committee.

Clinical IT Governance

Since so much money is now being spent on clinical systems, many hospitals and health systems have established specific structures and processes for clinical IT governance. The need for clinical IT governance is made even more important because of the key role that physicians play in the governance and success of health organizations.

EJGH has a clinical operations committee (COC) that is chaired by the CMIO and includes the chief nursing executive, the medical director, the chief of staff, nursing vice presidents, other physicians and IT staff. Under the COC are three subcommittees. The first is the physicians advisory committee, which is chaired by the CMIO. The second is the Meaningful Use steering committee. The third is the COMPASS advisory committee (COMPASS is EJGH's EHR system), which is composed of nurses. The hospital has shared governance, so nurses chair this committee, with the director of nursing informatics as the facilitator. The members are staff nurses and not nurse managers. They are selected because they are leaders among the nurses and have experience using the IT systems. The COMPASS advisory committee looks at all elements of proposed systems that would affect nursing. They also receive comments from nurses about existing systems and make recommendations about how to provide training on new systems.

Saint Luke's Health System has a clinical applications prioritization group chaired by the CMO and comprised of:
• One physician representative from each metropolitan facility, as appointed by the medical executive board of the respective facility, with input from the CMO, for a term of three years.
• The chief nursing officers from each of the metro facilities and the system CNO.
• The CMIO (ex officio).
• A senior IT representative (ex officio).
• The corporate controller (ex officio).

As described earlier, the system's management committee has delegated the function of assessing and prioritizing clinical applications to the clinical applications prioritization group.

EMHS has a clinical coordinating committee composed of the CMO, the CNO and the president of the medical staff of each member organization. There is a subcommittee of the clinical coordinating committee, the clinical systems steering committee, delegated to make design decisions about the EMR, the Cerner Millennium system. There is also a decision support work group composed of physicians that makes decisions on order sets and clinical pathways.

EMHS has an additional governance process for eQuest, the initiative to meet Meaningful Use requirements and receive federal stimulus funds. There is a steering committee that is chaired by EMHS's chief medical officer and includes the chief medical officers and chief nursing officers of each organization, eQuest medical director and nursing director, CIO, a human resources representative and a physician practice representative.

CIO and IT Staff Roles

The CIO's role is to educate and lead the technology discussions and decisions. The CIO knows the vendors best and should lead selections. CIOs must think strategically and be game changers or they will be replaced.
            —David L. Miller, Vice Chancellor and Chief Information Officer,
                University of Arkansas for Medical Sciences, Little Rock, AR

One of the primary roles of the CIO is organizational change management. Technology is just one of the tools to get there. If you don't use governance as part of that change manage-

---

Lutheran Health Network Clinical IT Governance

CLIC: Clinical Informatics Committee
- Physician lead, reports to medical executive committees.
- CMIOs, physician champions, CNOs, pharmacy, registration, clinical IT leadership.

Clinical Informatics Committee Expected Outcomes
- Review clinical system implementation status, issues, upcoming events and outstanding questions and concerns.
- Make decisions on behalf of the medical staffs.
- Facilitate communication with the medical staffs.
- Identify areas for improvement with the vendor and Lutheran Health Network leadership in utilizing clinical IT for improvements in safety, quality and clinical efficiency.

Source: Matthew J. Sprunger, MD, FACOG, and Mrunal S. Shah. Uncommon Knowledge: The Secrets Behind Effective IT Governance. HIMSS11. Available at www.himss.org/content/files/proceedings/2011/8.pdf. Accessed July 21, 2011.

---

ment, you're losing an opportunity. In the governance process, the CIO's role is structuring the process and the mechanics, whether it's meetings or materials. Also, the CIO staffs meetings, makes sure the participants are comfortable with the materials and facilitates meaningful discussion.

Governance isn't just one committee. There's very high-level governance and governance at the project level. The CIO needs to not only invite them to talk, but give them thoughtful content through presentations or one-on-one discussions. For example, we want a discussion of what comes next after the epic EMR installation. We need more than one group to discuss the issues facing IT.

—Eric Yablonka, Vice President and Chief Information Officer,
University of Chicago Medical Center, Chicago, IL

Jim Burton, CIO at EJGH, believes the CIO is both a facilitator and a driver. "I don't believe my decision is necessarily the best and want to be challenged. I am a catalyst," Burton says. The CIO sets boundaries such as how often to meet, but the decisions are made by the leadership. The CIO is an educator, bringing information on trends to the decision makers.

Cathy Bruno, CIO at EMHS, believes her role is "creating the process and then building the coalitions for its success." She looks at the issues, decides what needs to be solved and then develops proposals. "And then we sell it. And modify it as we go around if somebody has a better idea," Bruno says.

Is the CIO Giving up Authority by Creating a Governance Structure?

Giving up authority? That assumes you have authority and that I can tell the organization what they need to do. There are many influencers in the organization, including the CIO. To own IT as CIO is passé in the sense that the spend for IT must be owned by the organization. The CIO needs to let go of authority and allow the business side to own it. It's my role to help them understand the value of IT, but if they want to spend less, that's their decision. Given the future of healthcare, there are a lot of choices to be made and they have to be made by the leaders of the organization. Large dollar investments are involved as well as risks. These investments include EMRs and health information exchanges. The leadership has to decide what they want to invest and what kind of value they want to create and how they want to mitigate risk.

—Eric Yablonka, Vice President and Chief Information Officer,
University of Chicago Medical Center, Chicago, IL

Cathy Bruno, CIO at EMHS, feels she is not giving up authority in creating the governance process. "I have to build a coalition anyway and I'm not all-knowing," Bruno says. "It's very powerful to have an IS governance committee. I can say, 'You have to develop a business plan because the IS governance committee wants it.' The CEO chairs the governance committee. It gives me a lever. It gives me a way to say to the organization there is a process and it is supported by the organization. I don't see how in a complex organization where there are decisions that are conflicting that I could just decide. Our process is very collaborative."

CIO Staff Roles

The CIO's staff supports the various committees by, for example:

- Being responsible for preparation or overseeing preparation of proposals.
- Accepting requests reviewed for completeness prior to the meeting.
- Sending meeting packages in advance.
- Taking and distributing minutes.

Conclusion

In this chapter we have attempted to provide guidance on the essential elements of a committee structure and point out some issues to consider in creating that structure. Selecting members so that the committee represents the major stakeholders is critically important, but so is the willingness of members to devote time to the process. Defining the role of the CEO and CIO is particularly important. The number of committees and the roles they perform can be different to fit the needs of the governance process in a particular organization. In Chapter 4, we turn to the question of what processes and workflows should be created to support the work of committees in the governance process.

Chapter 4

Governance Processes and Workflows

IT governance requires the definition of a process for project proposal, review, prioritization, approval and management. This process is often closely related to the capital budgeting process, especially in terms of the time line for project approval. A workflow is defined for the involved committees. For example, project sponsors may be required to submit proposals at specific times to allow consideration by advisory committees in order to provide recommendations to the IT governance committee. The IT governance committee is then mandated to propose projects for the capital budgeting process by a specific date. Below are the processes and workflows that need to be designed as well as information on how the three hospitals and systems studied (see Chapters 6 through 8) carry them out.

Define a Governance Process

Although each hospital and health system has its own approach to IT governance, the following describes a typical process. The governance committee reviews all proposals that have already been reviewed by an advisory committee. Typically, there are three to four advisory committees, including committees for clinical services, business services and ambulatory care. These advisory committees review proposals to determine the benefits and quantify the return on investment. The governance committee then has to prioritize them for submission to the finance committee of the organization's board of directors.

The governance committee validates each project and determines whether the project should be done now or put in a future year's budget. The committee also has a role in ensuring that the project is completed on time and on budget. A project manager prepares both the budget and the time line, which then come to the governance committee for review and approval. A project manager provides the committee with regular reports as the project progresses.

Major projects, such as an institution-wide EHR system, frequently have a different process. A subcommittee with much broader representation might be formed that includes, for example, representatives of the medical school and a faculty practice. Responsibilities of this committee go beyond IT to implementation, operations and benefit realization. This subcommittee reports to the governance committee.

Workflow for Project Requests

Criteria are set to distinguish between a project that must move through the governance process and a service request that can go directly to the IT department. If the proposal meets the criteria for a project, a project request form must be completed by the sponsor. IT and finance staff will then review the request and help in developing additional information, such as initial and ongoing costs. A business case is prepared, and the proposal is then sent to the appropriate advisory committee for review. If the advisory committee approves, the proposal goes to the IT governance committee. The workflow and process for project assessment at EJGH in Metairie, Louisiana, is illustrated in Chapter 6.

Definition of a Project

If a project is not expected to require more than $10,000 and 80 hours of IT effort or to conflict with operations or approved projects, then the user and the IT department negotiate to schedule the project's execution. If any of the above parameters are exceeded, the CIO (or designee) and division VP (or designee) must determine if a business need exists to proceed with a business case.

At EMHS, the criterion for determining whether a potential project is subject to the governance process is whether it would require more than 400 hours of IT staff time. This criterion was developed by looking at past projects and using the 80/20 rule, or Pareto principle, that 80% of resources are consumed by 20% of events. The 20% of projects that require more than 400 hours of IT staff time were found to represent roughly 80% of the total IT hours used. This criterion reduces the number of proposals that the governance committee needs to review.

Project Request Forms

A common element in the project request processes at EJGH, Saint Luke's Health System and EMHS is the collaborative development of project requests and business cases. IT staff and staff from the finance departments get involved. An important question is how soon that should happen. If sponsors are allowed to gather information by themselves, the concern is that they will become convinced of the accuracy and completeness of the information they have, making it difficult for IT and finance staff to convince them that their information is inaccurate or incomplete. On the other hand, early involvement requires IT and finance staff resources that may be in short supply because of other projects. All three organizations have decided on joint development of proposals. EJGH and EMHS maintain a list of project ideas that are tracked before a formal project request is submitted or a business plan is prepared. EMHS has delegated responsibility for tracking that list to a member services unit, freeing the project management office to work on projects that are being implemented.

At Saint Luke's Health System, an IT prioritization request worksheet must be completed by the project sponsor. The worksheet requests the following:

- A description of the project.
- Five-year capital costs.
- Five-year operational costs.
- Projected operating cost savings (including full-time equivalent).
- A resource estimate for project completion.
- Project justification and linkage to strategic plan.
- Administrator approval.

A more complete description of the request worksheet is illustrated in the Saint Luke's Health System case study (Chapter 8). It includes major elements of a business case, such as five-year costs and benefits for the project.

At Saint Luke's Health System, the CIO solicits requests for new IT projects approximately 90 days prior to when the IT capital budget is due. To present a project proposal to a prioritization committee, the project sponsor must follow specific guidelines:

- A business plan is required.
- There must be agreement among peers that the project is important. If it is a system-wide project, the sponsor has to have gotten the approval of relevant people from other facilities. For example, to propose a system-wide radiology project, the head of radiology at one facility must obtain approval from all the other radiology department heads. The cost gets allocated to all facilities.
- The project must have an executive sponsor—someone who is on the management committee.
- There must be staff available in the department to do the work involved.

At EMHS a more detailed form is required, but it is prepared in stages with the assistance of both a project manager and IT staff. An initial request form is completed then the sponsor is interviewed. Finally, IS staff gather information on the requirements of the proposal. The final product is a business case for the project. The initial project request form is an Excel spreadsheet that asks about:

- Strategic alignment: the project's relation to the strategic pillars and related goals and objectives.
- The affected or interested business unit and departments within the unit.
- The proposed time line and drop-dead date.
- Critical and ideal outcomes.
- Related work already occurring or planned.
- Total labor and capital budget.
- Benefits with targets (e.g., increase operating efficiency by 10%) and measures.
- Whether a solution has been identified and whether it replaces a system.
- Whether it requires additional hardware or software.
- Whether it requires an interface to an existing system.

- Who will be responsible for maintenance?
- If information is contained that would be subject to HIPAA security requirements.
- Whether the project is discretionary or nondiscretionary.
- Authorization of a department head and executive sponsor.

Prepare a Business Case

Saint Luke's Health System, EJGH and EMHS all require business cases for larger projects. At EJGH, a business case includes:
- Heading: date, project name and champion(s)
- Description of business need
- Linkage to the IT and/or organizational strategic plan
- Description of solution and justification
- Benefits
- Cost and source of funding
- Constraints and assumptions
- Alternatives
- Timeline (requested start/end or duration)
- Forecasted IT resource availability and impact on other projects
- Return on investment

At EJGH, those requests agreed to by the CIO and a division VP must have a business case developed. The requesting business unit, IT, and the financial planning and analysis unit in the finance division jointly develop the business case. Financial planning and analysis will assist sponsors in preparing proposals and will review vendor cost information. Typically, they prepare the cost estimates for sponsors and the ROI for the business case. They question the assumptions that are being used. As noted earlier, the detailed project request form contains many of the elements of a business case. This is also true for Saint Luke's Health System (see Chapter 8).

At Saint Luke's Health System, the sponsor takes the lead in writing a business case. IT staff will also define the infrastructure and integration needed and the IT staff hours required. IT staff review the requests to ensure that the IT cost estimates and technical requirements are understood and not over- or underinflated. The corporate controller reviews the financial projections and agrees or disagrees with them. Requests are then compiled and delivered one week in advance to the prioritization group members for review prior to the meeting to discuss requests.

At EMHS, business cases are prepared for all projects that are projected to require more than 400 hours of IS department staff time. As described earlier, business cases are prepared jointly by the project sponsors and IS staff.

Require Project Sponsors Who Are Accountable

Every project should have a business sponsor who is not part of IT. The only time it should be an IT staff member is when it is an IT operations or infrastructure project. As discussed in Chapter 1, this is to confirm that it is a business unit, not IT, that owns and is accountable for the project.

The business sponsor brings the project to the advisory committee, and the IT governance committee then follows it during implementation with the help of a project manager. The project manager monitors the project, but it is the project sponsor who is accountable. For larger projects, the project sponsor provides the IT governance committee with a final report indicating whether the project was completed, whether it was on time and on budget and what modifications were made.

EMHS and Saint Luke's Health System both require a project sponsor and an executive sponsor. At Saint Luke's, the executive sponsor must be a member of the system management committee composed of senior executives of the system and CEOs of member facilities. The purpose is to ensure that sponsors will receive support during the implementation process and to create accountability for project success at senior levels of the organization.

Project Prioritization

EJGH, EMHS and Saint Luke's Health System use some of the same criteria but differ in who does the prioritization of projects. This is made explicit by the names of their advisory committees and the roles given to those committees.

Process

Saint Luke's Health System's management committee has delegated some of the decision-making about what is critical to the organization to a clinical applications prioritization group and a business applications prioritization group. Those groups are expected to review project requests and business plans and send the management committee a prioritized list of projects. The CIO and her staff try to de-emphasize financial return on investment and how difficult the project will be for IT to implement when they ask the clinical prioritization group to prioritize a project. They want them to focus on the value of the project. The group has the financial numbers, but the discussion tends to be about value.

While the prioritization committees establish the priority of individual projects in a single year, Saint Luke's five-year IT strategic plan documents the priorities across multiple years. Saint Luke's holds an annual half-day executive planning retreat that is attended by all business unit operating executive officers (hospitals, medical group and alternative care businesses) and corporate leaders (CEO, CFO, CMO, CIO, HR, planning, etc.).

The session is chaired by the system CEO, SVP of strategic planning and CFO. The objectives are to set priorities for the year, determine available capital and operating funding, provide education on industry developments and define which major initiatives will receive funding.

After the system's strategic plan is developed, the CIO leads an effort to update the IT five-year strategic plan. The plan sets measurable three- to five-year goals and objectives that are necessary to achieve the desired future. The goals and objectives are structured in three areas: clinical, financial/administrative and infrastructure. The goals and objectives are linked to the five perspectives of a Balanced Scorecard: workforce availability, customer, growth, quality and financial.

EJGH has information management advisory committees (IMACs) that include the clinical operations committee (COC), business systems committee, revenue cycle action team and HIPAA and information security committee. The charter for these committees includes the tasks of prioritizing annual capital budget requests and giving recommendations to the information management steering committee.

The IS governance committee at EMHS has only one advisory group. The IS directors group provides input on policies and anything that is taken to the IS governance committee. The directors group provides a forum for the IS directors from each facility to discuss common issues, such as the different ways that facilities are handling personal portable devices. They also generate project requests but are not asked to prioritize projects. Since most capital expenditures are in the budgets of member hospitals, they do the prioritization. This is likely to change as nondiscretionary programs take up more of the system's resources (see the EMHS case study in Chapter 7).

Criteria

Criteria need to be established for project prioritization. Whether a project utilizes a product from a core vendor is a criterion used by EJGH, EMHS and Saint Luke's Health System.

Jim Burton, CIO at EJGH, believes that governance should be simplified by deciding on a philosophy to guide decisions and make them easier. At EJGH, the philosophy is that enterprise IT applications should be utilized first. "We signed an enterprise agreement with Cerner. We use their product unless they can't provide 80% of what we need," Burton explains. Rather than just saying that the hospital favors enterprise applications, Burton would like to develop specific criteria for assessing whether the enterprise application is suited for the tasks required. This would simplify and speed up the process.

The first criteria EJGH uses now are whether the application exists and whether there is a business need. Then, the question is whether a Cerner product is available, since the hospital receives a very significant discount. If a Cerner product exists and project sponsors want something else, they are asked to do an evaluation of both products in a business case. The sponsors have to define functions and features that would not be available in the Cerner product and how, as a result, the Cerner product would not meet their business needs. Another consideration is whether resources would have to be used to integrate the product that could be used elsewhere, for example, to meet Meaningful Use requirements.

Both Saint Luke's Health System and EMHS explicitly require project sponsors to describe how the project supports the system's strategies. At Saint Luke's Health System, the clinical applications prioritization group should consider patient safety and practice efficiency. The business applications prioritization group should consider customer/employee satisfaction and financial stability. EMHS has defined six strategic pillars and their related goals and objectives. The six pillars are people, quality, service, finance, growth and community.[47]

Communication

As discussed in Chapter 2, communication is the first key to successful IT governance. EJGH, EMHS and Saint Luke's Health System have all adopted formal ways to communicate about the governance process to increase acceptance and encourage positive participation. They all focus specifically on physicians, whose cooperation is especially needed because most major IT projects are currently clinical systems.

All three organizations use the CMIO and CMO to provide formal updates to physician governance and advisory groups. At Saint Luke's Health System, there is a physician leadership group made up of the medical staff officers from each facility. The group meets four or five times a year and CEOs come as well. The CMIO gives quarterly updates.

The CMIO of EJGH presents at the four quarterly meetings of the medical staff. He sends out e-mails describing major projects and weekly e-mails to physicians telling them about projects and progress toward meeting Meaningful Use requirements. There is a physician portal where information is provided. Townhall meetings were held for a while, but they were stopped because of poor attendance.

Erik Steele, CMO of EMHS, believes that to keep physicians engaged you need to provide multiple modes of communication. CMIO reports are formally on the agenda of medical staff meetings. Reminders are built into the EHR system. Steele observes, "You may need to call physicians, as well as send materials, to emphasize the importance of what they should be reading. If they miss a meeting, a staff member needs to follow up with them and tell them what happened to issues they care about. Their performance needs to be monitored." Eric Hartz, CMIO at Eastern Maine Medical Center (EMMC), notes, "Our philosophy is to flood them with information in every possible way you can think of. We have personal communication, paper and electronic newsletters, and attendance at departmental meetings. We try to make IT part of the agendas."

Relationship of IT Governance to the Budgeting Process

EJGH, EMHS and Saint Luke's Health System engage in some similar tasks in coordinating their budgeting and IT governance processes:

- Capital expenses are first classified as nondiscretionary or discretionary.
- Nondiscretionary expenses are those required to comply with government regulations or the requirements of accreditation organizations, infrastructure expenses considered essential and previously committed expenses required by contracts or for uncompleted projects. Nondiscretionary expenses are not sent for prioritization to advisory committees and are reviewed but not evaluated by the governance committee.
- An initial target for discretionary spending is then set by the CFO and CIO.
- A timeline is set for the governance committee to send a list of prioritized projects to the finance committee of the board.

The budget is built bottom up through the governance process. Funding is then requested.
—David L. Miller, Vice Chancellor and Chief Information Officer,
University of Arkansas for Medical Sciences, Little Rock, AR

Capital Budget

Each year, Judy Brown, EJGH's CFO, determines how much capital spending the hospital can afford. Since getting to Meaningful Use requires additional funding, she allocates money for that purpose. Then, she estimates what implementing ICD-10 will cost. She allows funds for other needs, such as device replacement, and includes an amount for unforeseen expenses. The finance committee of the board approves a preliminary budget. The information management steering committee (IMSC), the organization's IT governance committee, then prioritizes projects and brings the list back to the finance committee. The finance committee approves the budget, but sponsors are required to come back with justification for large projects. The finance committee does not prioritize projects that fall within the preliminary budget limits. The finance committee also puts aside money for strategic projects, and anyone can come before the committee and the board with a proposal.

The time horizon is different at Saint Luke's Health System. Deborah Gash, Saint Luke's CIO, is told what the IT capital budget will be for the next five years. After the prioritization process, she determines when projects will be done taking into consideration the money that has been budgeted. She brings her list to the management committee, whose members have the opportunity to change the list and begin some projects sooner. They can also decide to go to the finance committee to request more money to get more projects done. The management committee takes the entire system's capital budget to the board. There is no separate presentation for IT.

EMHS has a more decentralized process. Most of the capital spending comes from the budgets of member facilities. Most of the money comes from the largest facility,

EMMC. Cathy Bruno requests that EMMC include items needed by EMHS in their capital budget. A few items, such as a system-wide e-mail server, are in the EMHS budget. The EMHS board's finance committee approves all IT spending, both its capital and its operating budgets. There is no separate board oversight review of IT.

Operating Budget

EMHS and Saint Luke's Health System differ in how their operating and capital budgets are coordinated. The process is affected by the degree of centralization in decision making.

At Saint Luke's Health System, CIO Deborah Gash presents both a list of projects that have been prioritized by advisory committees and an operating budget that includes the impact of the proposed projects to the management committee. The management committee approves any increases in the operating budget. If project spending has too great an impact on the operating budget, some projects in the capital budget may be postponed.

At EMHS, because most capital expenditures are in the budgets of its member facilities, coordination of the system's IS operating budget and the capital budget is not part of a single process. Cathy Bruno, EMHS's CIO, proposes a total IS budget to the CFO, who determines the percentages allocated to each member facility after the board approves the budget. Expenditures related to meeting Meaningful Use requirements are allocated differently. If a facility did not have an application, it is charged on the basis of net revenue. So if EMMC had an application, it is not charged again.

The Need for a PMO or Project Managers

Larger organizations should have a project management office (PMO) that creates and disseminates project management procedures, assigns project managers to projects and prepares reports for the business sponsor and governance committee. Smaller organizations should hire or train staff to be project managers for IT projects. The ideal candidate should have extensive project experience or be a trained project manager (e.g., a Project Management Professional [PMP] certified by the Project Management Institute [www.pmi.org]). Local colleges and universities may also offer training.

Both EJGH and EMHS have created PMOs. Saint Luke's Health System has not, and asks managers of applications (e.g., the EHR system) to both support those applications and carry out the function of project manager for new projects. The rationale is described in Chapter 5.

Post-Implementation Review

For the largest projects, some organizations may require the sponsor to return to the governance committee in 6 to 18 months following completion to describe whether the project actually provided the benefits that were expected. This allows the committee to assess its own work.

None of the three organizations studied do this consistently. The CIO at EJGH and the CEO of EMHS both feel this is not the appropriate responsibility of an IT governance committee. They believe accountability for achieving the benefits rests with the management of the sponsoring unit.

Jim Burton, CIO at EJGH, believes it is not the responsibility of the governance committee and the IT governance process to determine whether the business sponsors got the benefits they wanted. The governance process controls only the technology. "We are not the business process architects," Burton says. "We are not running a department. We don't hire the people. There are so many elements that governance doesn't control." Governance focuses on whether the technology provided the benefits that were expected.

For high-dollar projects, the finance committee at EJGH will sometimes ask for a review of benefits, including return on investment, six months after implementation. There is also an audit committee of the board that will review IT audits, for example, a security and HIPAA audit.

At Saint Luke's Health System, the management committee operates as the governance committee for IT. Because the management committee is the executive committee for the entire system, doing a post-implementation review is considered appropriate. There is no requirement for projects to be reviewed after implementation to determine whether the benefits have been received. Some projects have been reviewed, but size was not the primary determining factor. It was the magnitude of the change involved.

Frameworks: COBIT and ITIL®

Frameworks have been developed that are widely used to define the necessary steps and procedures for effective IT governance. Two of them are COBIT[48] and ITIL®.[49] These frameworks serve as guides to how governance should be carried out. Since they have been developed by experts and carefully reviewed, they provide detailed and thorough guidelines.

COBIT

COBIT (Control Objectives for Information and related Technology) was developed by the Information Systems Audit and Control Association (ISACA). It defines processes and standards for IT governance. For example, it suggests the creation of a RACI chart that identifies who is responsible, accountable, consulted and/or informed about IT processes. Figure 4-1 is a RACI chart for defining an IT strategic plan and illustrates why COBIT is useful. The user is asked to think about the difference between, for example, being consulted and being informed. COBIT promotes a disciplined approach to developing policies by creating a matrix that needs to be completed, making it difficult to forget to define the decision rights of a particular stakeholder.

RACI Chart	Functions	CEO	CFO	Business Executive	CIO	Business Process Owner	Head Operations	Chief Architect	Head Development	Head IT Administration	PMO	Compliance Audit Risk and Security
Activities												
Link business goals to IT goals.		C	I	A/R	R	C						
Identify critical dependencies and current performance.		C	C	R	A/R	C	C	C	C	C		C
Build an IT strategic plan.		A	C	C	R	I	C	C	C	C	I	C
Build IT tactical plans.		C	I		A	C	C	C	C	C	R	I
Analyse programme portfolios and manage project and service portfolios.		C	I	I	A	R	R	C	R	C	C	I

A RACI chart identifies who is Responsible, Accountable, Consulted and/or Informed.

Figure 4-1: RACI Chart. *Source: ISACA*[50]

For IT to be successful in delivering against business requirements, management should put an internal control system or framework in place. The COBIT control framework contributes to these needs by:
- Making a link to the business requirements.
- Organizing IT activities into a generally accepted process model.
- Identifying the major IT resources to be leveraged.
- Defining the management control objectives to be considered.

The business orientation of COBIT consists of linking business goals to IT goals, providing metrics and maturity models to measure their achievement and identifying the associated responsibilities of business and IT process owners.

The process focus of COBIT is illustrated by a process model that subdivides IT into four domains and 34 processes in line with the responsibility areas of plan, build, run and monitor, providing an end-to-end view of IT. Enterprise architecture concepts help identify the resources essential for process success, i.e., applications, information, infrastructure and people.[51]

IT control objectives provide a complete set of high-level requirements to be considered by management for effective control of each IT process. They:
- Are statements of managerial actions to increase value or reduce risk.
- Consist of policies, procedures, practices and organizational structures.
- Are designed to provide reasonable assurance that business objectives will be achieved and undesired events will be prevented or detected and corrected.[52]

Figure 4-2 provides examples of the business, IT, process and activity goal relationship. Figure 4-3 provides possible goal or outcome measures for the example in Figure 4-2. Figure 4-4 illustrates how outcome measures for the example become performance metrics.

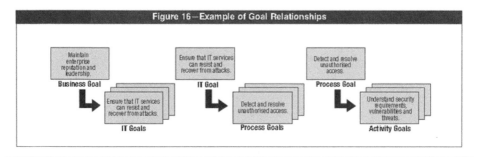

Figure 4-2: Business, IT, Process and Activity Goal Relationship.
Source: ISACA[53]

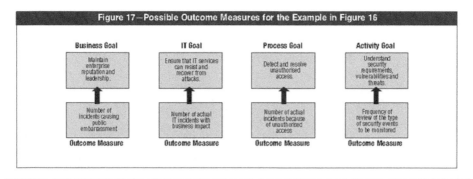

Figure 4-3: Possible Goal or Outcome Measures for Business, IT, Process
and Activity Goal Relationship. *Source: ISACA*[53]

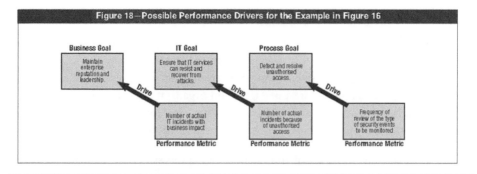

Figure 4-4: How Outcome Measures Become Performance Metrics.
Source: ISACA[53]

The COBIT 4.1 framework can be downloaded for free (registration required) at www.isaca.org/Knowledge-Center/cobit/Pages/Downloads.aspx.

ITIL

The Information Technology Infrastructure Library (ITIL) is another framework for IT governance and service management. ITIL was developed by the Office of Government Commerce (OGC), a part of the Efficiency and Reform Group of the Cabinet Office, a department of the Government of the United Kingdom. The ITIL best practices are detailed within five core guidance publications. Information is available at www.itil-officialsite.com/.

Chapter 5

IT Governance and Project Management

IT governance will not result in successful projects unless effective project management is in place. If the hospital or health system has created a project management office (PMO), the PMO manages product selection then stays involved through implementation. A PMO can assist the governance process by reporting on the entire portfolio of projects proposed and in progress to assist in project prioritization. Project managers can help define the project risks that must be considered in the governance process and help in mitigating them. Project managers and a PMO often take on the task of reporting progress to project sponsors and those responsible for governance. A closed-loop process is sometimes put in place which requires that project sponsors report to those responsible for governance on what the costs and realized benefits were for approved projects. The PMO can assist in assembling data for this process.

Requirements for Effective Project Management

Effective project management requires integration with the governance process. IT governance defines who is responsible and accountable for the success of a project—necessary information for project managers. Governance sets the priority of a project, which is needed for the management of resources.

Effective IT governance and project management are both necessary for completing projects that deliver benefits and are completed on time and on budget.

Relationship with the IT Governance Committee

In support of the governance committee, project managers develop and prepare reports on project status and budget. A standing item on the meeting agenda of the committee is the report from the PMO, if one exists. The PMO report typically depicts the schedule and budget status of each major project in development, provides summarized information on mid-size projects, presents information on IT budget performance and assembles other IT operational performance reports as requested.

PMO or Project Managers

Larger organizations should have a PMO that creates and disseminates project management procedures, assigns project managers to projects and prepares reports for the business sponsor and governance committee. Smaller organizations should hire or train staff to be project managers for IT projects. The ideal candidate should have extensive project experience or be a trained project manager (e.g., a Project Management Professional [PMP] certified by the Project Management Institute [www.pmi.org)]. Local colleges and universities may also offer training.

Project Manager Role

At EJGH, project managers help project sponsors develop a business case. After approval, a project charter is prepared. Chapter 6 illustrates the components of a project charter.

Project managers prepare a mini-scope that describes the high-level cost of the project, how long the project will take and the resources required. After the project is approved, they prepare a full-blown scope document. The business sponsor and the department head sign off on the scope.

Project managers then provide the information to keep the project on time and on budget. Comparing projects is not their job.

PMO and Project Portfolio Management

Jim Burton, CIO at EJGH, believes that portfolio management is needed because there are interdependencies between projects. It helps make choices on the use of resources. The customer can make choices about how resources are used and see the trade-offs. The PMO manages all projects, not just those that go through the governance committee review process. The PMO should be contributing to capacity planning.

Cerner operates the PMO at EJGH and employs the project managers. The PMO manages non-Cerner projects. Matt MacVey, Cerner's site executive, describes the goal as getting to the point where they resource load all the project plans. They can then roll it up and look at those resources across the entire organization. "We're trying to get to the point where there is a defined time line for proposing a project as part of the budgetary cycle so we can look at the entire portfolio of projects before a decision is made," MacVey explains.

When the EJGH IT governance committee first approves a project, it is approving the funding, not a specific start date. The CIO comes back to the committee with a time line after reviewing with the PMO the other projects that are being implemented. Burton provides the committee a spreadsheet with information about all the projects and asks for decisions about which ones should proceed and which should be delayed.

Burton believes that, "Portfolio management is a wasted exercise unless you're within 10% of scope." He believes that portfolio management will improve as the discipline of governance is accepted and methodologies are applied.

The PMO has created and tracks an idea list of the projects under consideration for which no scope document or business case has been prepared. MacVey feels that "if we don't do this, people develop their own set of data about why we should do the project." It is then difficult to persuade them to look at other data.

At EMHS, the PMO is part of what is called the client care collaborative, which also includes business operations and member services. EMHS has divided the responsibility for managing projects. The PMO is responsible for projects that are being implemented. Member services is responsible for managing project ideas or requests. When a project request is made, staff from member services interview the proposer to get more details. They engage in progressive elaboration of the proposal, asking a series of questions to determine both the needs and the scope of the project. Member services does not want to move forward and develop specifications for a project that costs over $1 million when the sponsor is interested in a project that costs $100,000.

In regard to governance, business operations is responsible for data acquisition and reporting on the operations of the IS department, including reporting to the IT Governance Committee. Project status reports are prepared and disseminated by the PMO.

A project and portfolio management tool is used by EMHS to track three portfolios. Like EJGH, EMHS records and tracks project ideas. The discovery portfolio contains ideas for projects. The business portfolio includes projects that are being implemented. The foundation portfolio includes the support projects that maintain the current systems. The items in the discovery portfolio are tracked to determine if member ideas have moved to the next stage or there is a need to discuss what happened.

An Alternative to the PMO

Saint Luke's Health System has not created a PMO and does not engage in what IS staff explicitly call project portfolio management. Instead, Saint Luke's uses a five-year strategic plan to manage the project portfolio and merges the roles of project manager and application support.

If a project is included in the IT five-year plan, success measures are identified, a time line for deployment is developed and a customer sponsor and IT project manager are named to oversee progress in deployment. Action plans, including coordination of resources, are developed in accordance with an IT project management methodology. The project is then reported on and tracked. The current status of all projects is available on an intranet. This includes major milestones of each project.

Action plans are prepared and reviewed quarterly by IT staff. There is a document that lists all of the projects that will be undertaken that year. The CIO meets with IT staff and presents a plan for the next quarter for completing the projects. If projects are not on target, a plan is presented to get back on target. That information is shared with the various user groups.

Todd Hatton, Saint Luke's chief applications officer, points out, "We use the principles of the PMO, but we don't have a formal PMO." His division has program managers assigned to each customer segment, such as clinical and finance. They are responsible for all applications in their areas. Each program manager supervises a group of project managers who have a staff of analysts. Each unit does the application support as well as the implementation for new projects. "We have not split the teams so that one unit does only production support and another does new projects," Hatton explains. "A project manager could be supporting an existing application while working on a new project. The advantage of this is that it is very clear who the owner of an application is. The customer knows who to go to."

IT has developed a project management methodology. Analysts and project managers are taught project management skills such as the meaning of lag time and how to develop a scope document.

The staff are experts in the applications they support. "We don't have the project management mentor role—an individual who helps teach others how to do project management," Hatton adds.

Chapter 6

Case Study: *IT Governance at East Jefferson General Hospital, Metairie, LA*

Introduction

East Jefferson General Hospital (EJGH) in Metairie, Louisiana, opened in 1971. EJGH started as a 250-bed facility with almost 250 physicians serving the newly burgeoning suburbs of Jefferson Parish. From the beginning, the hospital was to be a not-for-profit community hospital with a board of directors comprised of representatives from the community's financial, educational, civic, and business community. Today, EJGH stands as a state-of-the-art hospital with more than 420 beds. Still a community hospital with a board comprised of representatives throughout the community, our patients are served by a staff of more than 3,000 team members and more than 650 physicians.

—EJGH Fact Sheet (www.ejgh.org)

Jim Burton, EJGH's Senior Vice President and CIO, arrived 18 months ago and has worked with the hospital's leadership to improve governance. The number of projects implemented and completed on time and on budget has increased. He believes IT has a respect that it did not have before.

Purpose of IT Governance

Burton believes the purpose of IT governance is to help the customer—senior leadership, clinicians and business sponsors—make the right choices. The value of governance is good decisions and also good methodologies.

He believes that governance is not just about getting decisions, it is about educating people. Upon arrival, Burton was able to focus on infrastructure, such as the wireless network, because he educated the steering committee about the need for focusing on it rather than on individual projects people presented—the quick wins. Governance removes a lot of the pressure on IT to respond to individual demands.

Burton feels that a successful governance process leaves people feeling that they had a voice. They understand why decisions were made. "People are willing to comply

53

because they see that we are successful, that applications are being implemented," says Burton.

Committee Structure
Information Management Steering Committee
The information management steering committee (IMSC) is a decision-making body composed of senior management team members, responsible for defining and providing guidance in the development, funding and support of the organization's corporate information management policy framework. The committee defines the information management framework via an Information Management Strategic Plan. The committee monitors progress made against the plan through the use of various management reporting tools.

The information management steering committee is chaired by the CIO but with the CEO as the executive sponsor. Members include the CFO, CMIO, medical director, chief nursing executive, vice president of marketing, vice president of business development and vice president of outpatient services. The IMSC meets monthly. "Keeping people engaged and attending meetings has not been a problem because they know decisions will be made and followed through," Burton explains.

All the members of the committee are permanent members, but other people come in to present projects or supply information and advice. For example, members of the legal department will be pulled in when the need arises.

The IMSC sets executive policy on EJGH information management topics. It reviews, recommends as appropriate and monitors major EJGH information management initiatives. The IMSC has final decision-making authority on IM strategic proposals and proposals of operational significance, monitors IM strategic metrics (e.g., key accomplishments, capital budget, SLAs) and approves recommendations for changes. The IMSC approves the IT/IM strategic plan and associated capital budgets. It is charged with assuring that the IT/IM strategic plan is aligned to the organization's strategic plan. It monitors relevant strategic performance metrics that information management contributes, and provides regular IM updates to the appropriate board committee(s).

Advisory Committees
Four permanent advisory committees report up to the IMSC. The first committee to organize under the IMSC was the clinical operations committee (COC), which is chaired by the CMIO and includes the chief nursing executive, medical director, chief of staff, nursing vice presidents, other physicians and IT staff.

The next committee organized was the business systems committee, which is chaired by the CFO and includes representatives from materials management, human resources, accounting, marketing, legal and IT. There is also a revenue cycle action team (RCAT), which is chaired by the CFO and includes revenue cycle directors. Judy Brown, EJGH's executive vice president and CFO, believes these committees and the governance process give staff in the business services and revenue cycle areas greater confidence that they are being heard.

There is also a HIPAA and information security committee (HISC), which is chaired by the CIO and includes representation from compliance, legal, nursing, physicians and IT. There is also an IT infrastructure committee.

Each committee works on issues that are brought to them or are raised by their members, including project and budget decisions. Once they are in agreement, or if they cannot agree, the issue is brought to the IMSC for disposition.

The COC brings together physicians and nurses, which did not occur before Burton's arrival. Under the COC are three subcommittees. One is the Physicians Advisory Committee (PAC), which is chaired by the CMIO. There is also a Meaningful Use Steering Committee, which will continue to meet as long as federal Meaningful Use requirements must be met to receive federal incentive payments.

The third is the CAC or COMPASS Advisory Committee (COMPASS is EJGH's EHR system), which is composed of nurses. The hospital has shared governance, so nurses chair the committee, with the director of nursing informatics as the facilitator. The members are staff nurses and not nurse managers. They are selected because they are leaders among the nurses and have experience using the IT systems. The CAC looks at all elements of proposed systems that would affect nursing and receives comments from nurses about existing systems. They give recommendations on how to provide training on new systems.

There are also application-level subcommittees, such as the one for Cerner Millennium systems. The basic distinction is between clinical and business applications. Burton believes EJGH is not big enough to need a separate committee for each clinical area, for example, ambulatory care.

Business sponsors will usually bring projects first to an advisory committee because they are already represented there. The advisory committee will send projects forward to the IMSC, but may request revisions from the sponsor. The IMSC has also sent proposals back to the advisory committee for further clarification. The advisory committees can reject and are expected to reject some proposals.

Governance Processes and Workflows
Communication with Physicians

The CMIO presents at the four quarterly meetings of the medical staff. He sends out e-mails describing major projects and weekly e-mails to physicians telling them about projects and progress toward meeting Meaningful Use requirements. There is a physician portal where information is provided. Townhall meetings were held for a while, but they were stopped because of poor attendance.

Policies and Procedures

Figure 6-1 contains EJGH's policies and procedures for IT governance.

East Jefferson General Hospital Metairie, La 70006 Title: **INFORMATION MANAGEMENT** **GOVERNANCE COMMITTEES** Reviewed: 10/95; 10/98; 10/01; 8/04 Revised: 3/04; 8/05; 7/07; 11/10	Administrative Policy & Procedure Policy No: IT-2 Page 1 of 6 Effective Date: September 15, 1983 Approved by: ORIGINAL SIGNED BY DR. PETERS Dr. Mark Peters, MD, President and CEO

I.   POLICY:

The Information Management Governing Committees are charged with defining and guiding the organization's corporate information management program. The framework seeks to facilitate the efficient, effective and strategic use of information and enabling technologies in a manner that supports the organization's strategies, tactics, and objectives.

II.   DEPARTMENTS AFFECTED:

All Hospital Departments, Medical Staff, and Volunteers

III. DEFINITIONS:

Information Management (IM): The functions and processes employed by an organization to obtain, manage and use information to enhance and improve individual and organizational performance in patient care, governance, management and support processes.

Information Technology (IT): The organizational structures within EJGH required to maintain and support the communications network, infrastructure (hardware) and applications (software) of EJGH.

Information Management Strategic Plan (IMSP): A plan that provides specific direction in the ongoing development and implementation of information management processes, practices, and technologies within the organization. Specific direction is conveyed in the form of strategies, tactics, objectives, and where appropriate, specific goals or projects. The plan is tightly aligned to the organization's business strategic plan.

Information Management Steering Committee (IMSC): A decision-making body composed of senior management Team Members, responsible for defining and providing guidance in the development, funding and support of the organization's corporate information management policy framework. The committee defines the information management framework via an Information Management Strategic Plan. The committee monitors progress made against the plan through the use various management reporting tools.

FIGURE 6-1: EJGH's IT Governance Policies and Procedures

East Jefferson General Hospital
Metairie, La 70006

Administrative Policy & Procedure
Policy No: IT-2
Page 2 of 6

Title: **INFORMATION MANAGEMENT GOVERNANCE COMMITTEES**

Information Management Advisory Committees (IMACs): Decision-making bodies authorized by IMSC to oversee a specific aspect of Information Management use comprised of management Team Members involved in the day-to-day operations of the Hospital to which data, information, associated technologies and information processes lends support.

Program: A group of related projects and operational activities coordinated in a way to obtain benefits and control not available from managing them individually.

Project: A temporary endeavor undertaken to create a unique product, service or result.

IV. INFORMATION MANAGEMENT STEERING COMMITTEE (IMSC) SCOPE AND DUTIES:

A. The Information Management Steering Committee (IMSC) shall review IMACs' usefulness annually, adjust as necessary, and appoint the leader of each chartered committee. Participation will be adjusted to meet organizational and staff changes.

B. Sets executive policy on EJGH Information Management topics.

C. Reviews, recommends as appropriate, and monitors major EJGH Information Management initiatives.

D. Final decision making on IM strategic proposals and those of operational significance; monitors IM strategic metrics (e.g. key accomplishments, capital budget, SLA's) and approves recommendations for changes.

E. Final decision-making on unbudgeted project requests costing more than $10,000 or more than 80 hours of effort up to the limits of the highest ranking executive participating as specified by Administrative Policy MM-4 Principle Purchasing Policy. Provides recommendation to next level authority for projects exceeding those limits. (Reference Administrative Policy MM-4 Principal Purchasing Policy for authorization limits by position of budgeted and unbudgeted purchases.)

In the event of urgent business matters, a special meeting comprised of the Chief Financial Officer (CFO), Chief Information Officer (CIO), Chief Nursing Officer (CNO) or Chief Medical Information Officer (CMIO) and one other Chief Officer member of the IMSC (or any of their designated representatives) may be conducted to review the project(s). This group will act as a subset of the IMSC to make approval decisions up to the authority of the highest ranking executive

FIGURE 6-1: *(continued)*

East Jefferson General Hospital
Metairie, La 70006

Administrative Policy & Procedure
Policy No: IT-2
Page 3 of 6

Title: **INFORMATION MANAGEMENT
GOVERNANCE COMMITTEES**

participating. All decisions made by this IMSC Sub-group will be reported back
to the entire IMSC membership at the next regularly scheduled meeting.

F.   Prioritizes projects and resources where IMAC conflicts occur, approves system
selections, performance metrics and budgets.

G.   Approves the IT/IM strategic plan, and associated capital budgets.

H.   Assures that the IT/IM strategic plan is aligned to the organization's strategic
plan.

I.   Monitors relevant strategic performance metrics that Information Management
contributes.

J.   Provides regular IM updates to the appropriate Board committee(s).

V.   **INFORMATION MANAGEMENT STEERING COMMITTEE STRUCTURE:**

The Information Management Steering Committee shall be composed of the following
members:

A.   Chief Executive Officer

B.   Executive Vice President/Chief Operating Officer

C.   Chief Financial Officer

D.   Chief Nursing Executive

E.   Chief Medical Officer or similar position

F.   Chief Medical Informatics Officer

G.   Chief Information Officer (Chairman)

H.   Vice-President of Marketing

I.   Vice-President of Business Development

J.   Vice-President Outpatient Services

FIGURE 6-1: *(continued)*

East Jefferson General Hospital
Metairie, La 70006

Administrative Policy & Procedure
Policy No: IT-2
Page 4 of 6

Title: **INFORMATION MANAGEMENT
GOVERNANCE COMMITTEES**

VI.   MEETING FREQUENCY:

IMSC will meet at least <u>monthly.</u>

A meeting agenda will be prepared by the Chief Information Officer and minutes will be taken.

**VII.   INFORMATION MANAGEMENT ADVISORY COMMITTEES (IMACs) SCOPE
AND DUTIES:**

A.   Reviews and makes recommendations to IMSC for Information Management (IM) projects with costs over $10,000 or over 80 hours of effort, or where a project request will cause resource constraints requiring priority adjustments. Examples of past and present IMACs include the Clinical Operations Committee (COC), the Revenue Cycle Action Team (RCAT), the IT Infrastructure Committee, and the HIPAA and Information Security Committee (HISC).

B.   Provides advice to the Chief Information Officer (CIO) and Information Management Steering Committee on strategic proposals, project evaluations, priorities (projects and/or operations), project/system selections, and budgets. Prioritizes annual capital budget requests, sets the annual project schedule, and handles competing resource requests for their area of focus.

C.   Reviews "IT-impactable" performance metrics (e.g. SLA's, Project dashboard, Monthly dashboard, accomplishments) and participates in the design of improvements where appropriate.

D.   Reviews and approves requests that impact the ability of IT to meet business goals. Approves, monitors and facilitates the start, progress, and completion of active IM change requests. Shares in the responsibility of project outcomes, including testing where necessary.

E.   Ensures that recommended projects are properly aligned to the area's annual and/or strategic plan, IM strategic plan and tactical goals of EJGH.

F.   Provides advice to IT to meet operational goals.

G.   Guides IT's direction in line with external governance (HIPAA, FDA, TJC, etc.)

H.   Reviews IT risk assessments and recommendations, monitors risks, and may request an audit to validate risk levels.

FIGURE **6-1:** *(continued)*

East Jefferson General Hospital
Metairie, La 70006

Administrative Policy & Procedure
Policy No: IT-2
Page 5 of 6

Title: **INFORMATION MANAGEMENT
GOVERNANCE COMMITTEES**

I.   Reviews IT related incidents (e.g. SLA's, downtimes) as applicable to their area of focus.

J.   Recommends and refers proposed changes to enterprise-wide (Administrative) policies and procedures as needed.

K.   Oversees the education of EJGH Team Members on IM initiatives and activities.

L.   Provides positive support to information and technology groups.

M.   Recommends staff to participate in the evaluation, selection, or implementation of systems.

N.   Disseminates information across the enterprise.

VIII.   **INFORMATION MANAGEMENT ADVISORY COMMITTEES STRUCTURE**:

Membership shall minimally include a non-IT leader who will co-chair each committee with the CIO or designee of the IT management team, unless the scope of the committee has no direct impact outside of IT (ex. IT Infrastructure Committee). The majority of attendees will be comprised of stakeholders.

IX.   **MEETING FREQUENCY:**

IMACs will meet at least monthly.

A meeting agenda will be prepared by the designated representative of each Committee and minutes will be taken.

X.   **INFORMATION MANAGEMENT GOVERNANCE STRUCTURE:**

See flowchart next page.

XI.   **RESPONSIBILITY:**

Questions concerning this policy and recommended revisions shall be directed to the Chief Information Officer (CIO) or designee.

XII.   **REFERENCES:**

Administrative Policies:
MM-4 Principal Purchasing Policy

FIGURE 6-1: *(continued)*

East Jefferson General Hospital
Metairie, La 70006

Administrative Policy & Procedure
Policy No: IT-2
Page 6 of 6

Title: **INFORMATION MANAGEMENT**
GOVERNANCE COMMITTEES

XIII. ATTACHMENTS:

P-9.01 IT PROJECT ASSESSMENT WORKFLOW

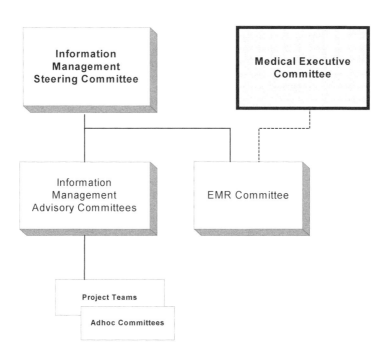

INFORMATION MANAGEMENT COMMITTEE GOVERNANCE STRUCTURE

FIGURE 6-1: *(continued)*

Workflow

Figure 6-2 shows the workflow for project assessment, and Figure 6-3 describes the process. If the project is not expected to require more than $10,000 and 80 hours of IT effort or to conflict with operations or approved projects, then the user and the IT department negotiate to schedule the project for execution. If any of those parameters are exceeded, the CIO (or designee) and division VP (or designee) must determine if a business need exists to proceed with a business case.

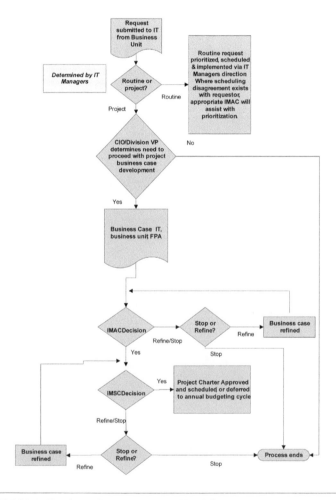

IT-2 Information Management Governance Committees
Attachment P-9.01 IT Project Assessment Workflow

FIGURE 6-2: EJGH's Project Assessment Workflow

IT-2 Information Management Governance Committees
Attachment P-9.01

IT PROJECT ASSESSMENT WORKFLOW DESCRIPTION

Request submitted to IT
- ❏ Requests are submitted to IT via the IT Customer Service Center (Call Center), a phone call, in person, etc.

Routine or Project
- ❏ If the project is expected to not require more than $10,000, 80 hours of effort, or conflict with operations or approved projects, then the user and the IT department(s) negotiate to schedule the project for execution.

- ❏ If any of the above parameters are exceeded, then the CIO (or designee) and division VP (or designee) must determine if a business need exists to proceed with a business case.

Business Case Development

- ❏ Those requests agreed to by the CIO and division VP must have a business case developed. See Appendix A for a component template.
- ❏ The requesting business unit, IT, and Financial Planning and Analysis jointly develop the business case.
- ❏ Responsibilities: business unit: clarify business need, IT: estimate durations, resources, and costs, FPA: create ROI.

Approval Outside of Annual Budgeting Process
Requests submitted outside the budgeting cycle will be considered in compelling cases such as:
1) Initiative is necessary to achieve a strategic goal
2) Initiative is required for regulatory compliance
3) Existing functionality is no longer adequate to support hospital operations
4) Initiative would provide hospital with significant return-on-investment ROI

FIGURE 6-3: EJGH's Description of Project Assessment Workflow

Each request agreed to by the CIO and division VP must have a business case developed. The requesting business unit, IT, and the financial planning and analysis unit in the finance division jointly develop the business case. Financial planning and analysis will assist sponsors in preparing proposals and will review vendor cost information. Typically, they prepare the cost estimates for sponsors and the ROI for the business case. They question the assumptions that are being used.

While all projects must go to the IMSC, there is a process for making decisions between meetings for projects that are required for compliance or to deal with an immediate need. The governance policies and procedures allow the CIO, CFO and CEO to approve such projects, which are then presented at the next IMSC meeting.

Unbudgeted items can be approved by the CFO and CEO up to specified limits. For the CFO, the limit is $100,000, and the CEO can approve up to $250,000. Beyond those limits, the proposal must be presented to the finance committee of the board.

IT-2 Information Management Governance Committees
Attachment P-9.01

APPENDIX A

Components

Components for Business Case. Information needed for governance to make a sound decision.

- ❑ Heading: Date, Project Name, and Champion(s)
- ❑ Description of Business Need
- ❑ Linkage to the IT and/or Organizational Strategic Plan
- ❑ Description of Solution and Justification
- ❑ Benefits
- ❑ Cost and Source of Funding
- ❑ Constraints and Assumptions
- ❑ Alternatives
- ❑ Time Line (requested start/end or duration)
- ❑ Forecasted IT Resource Availability and Impact to Other Projects
- ❑ Return on Investment

Components for a Project Charter. Document granting organizational authority to the project manager to proceed with the project.

- ❑ What is the project goal, scope, and key deliverables?
- ❑ Who is the project manager?
- ❑ What level of authority does he/she have?
- ❑ Who are the required members of the project team?
- ❑ What are the requirements for success?
- ❑ Next steps for project organization and timeframe.
- ❑ Call for commitment from necessary stakeholders.
- ❑ What are the time expectations (start, finish)?

FIGURE 6-3: *(continued)*

This is just to secure the funds. The project must still be evaluated by the IMSC in terms of its relationship to other projects and the dependencies involved.

Project Prioritization

Business cases are prepared for all projects that meet the criteria for review by the IMSC. Table 6-1 describes the components of a business case.

Jim Burton believes that governance should be simplified by deciding on a philosophy and set of criteria. There has to be a philosophy that guides decisions and makes them easier. At EJGH, the philosophy is that enterprise IT applications should be utilized first. "We signed an enterprise agreement with Cerner to use their product unless they can't provide 80% of what we need," Burton says. "Project sponsors who want a product not provided by the Cerner contract must explain why."

Table 6-1: Components for a Business Case
(Information needed for governance to make a sound decision)

1. Heading: Date, Project Name, and Champion(s)
2. Description of Business Need
3. Linkage to the IT and/or Organizational Strategic Plan
4. Description of Solution and Justification
5. Benefits
6. Cost and Source of Funding
7. Constraints and Assumptions
8. Alternatives
9. Time Line (requested start/end or duration)
10. Forecasted IT Resource Availability and Impact to Other Projects
11. Return on Investment

Burton wants to improve the governance process by creating more detailed and formal rules for how decisions are made. So rather than just saying that the hospital favors enterprise applications, he would like to see specific criteria for assessing whether an enterprise application is suited for the tasks required. That would simplify and speed up the process.

The first criteria now are whether the needed application exists and whether there is a business need. Then the question is whether a Cerner product is available, since the hospital receives a very significant discount. If a Cerner product exists and project sponsors want something else, they are asked to do an evaluation of both products in a business case. The sponsors have to define functions and features that would not be available in the Cerner product and how, as a result, the Cerner product would not meet their business needs. Another consideration is whether resources would have to be used to integrate the product that could be used elsewhere, for example, to meet Meaningful Use requirements.

Burton emphasizes, "In determining ROI, we consider people, process and technology. Will it improve the process? Will it optimize or reduce the number of people? Then, will it save money?"

Post-Implementation Review

The CIO shares the time line and budget for current and completed projects with the IMSC. Burton believes it is not the responsibility of the IMSC and the governance process to determine whether the business sponsors got the benefits they wanted. The governance process controls only the technology. "We are not the business process architects. We are not running a department. We don't hire the people. There are so many elements that governance doesn't control," Burton says. Governance focuses on whether the technology provided the benefits that were expected.

Relation to Budgeting

Jim Burton puts IT expenses into three categories. There are expenses that must be incurred because, for example, infrastructure is not working. Then there are expenses for contracts already signed, for example, the contract with Cerner. Then there are projects that are desirable and for which the IMSC needs to set priorities. The finance committee of the board makes the final decision.

During the meeting to decide on projects to present for the annual budget, projects are prioritized in the IMSC using anonymous voting. If projects are equally ranked, the CEO makes the final decision.

Each year, Judy Brown, EJGH's CFO, determines how much capital spending the hospital can afford. Since getting to Meaningful Use requires additional funding, she allocates money for that purpose. Then she estimates what implementing ICD-10 will cost. She allows funds for other needs, such as device replacement, and includes an amount for unforeseen expenses. The finance committee of the board approves a preliminary budget. The IMSC then prioritizes projects and brings the list back to the finance committee. The finance committee approves the budget, but sponsors are required to come back with justification for large projects. The finance committee does not prioritize projects that fall within the preliminary budget limits. They also put aside money for strategic projects, and anyone can come before the committee and the board with a proposal.

For high-dollar projects, the finance committee will sometimes ask for a review of benefits, including return on investment, six months after implementation. There is also an audit committee of the board that will review IT audits, for example, a security and HIPAA audit.

Executive Roles
CIO Role

Jim Burton believes that "IT doesn't drive governance, IT feeds governance." The CIO and his staff provide the methodologies and information that help the IMSC and board make decisions.

Burton believes the CIO is both a facilitator and a driver. "I don't believe my decision is the best and want to be challenged. I am a catalyst," he says. The CIO provides structure, such as how often to meet, but the decisions are made by the leadership. The CIO is an educator, bringing information about trends to the decision makers.

CEO and CFO Roles

The CEO and CFO are expected to attend all IMSC meetings. Jim Burton believes the role of the CEO is to "see the forest." The CEO is involved in decisions that are unrelated to IT but affect IT. Burton believes the role of the CFO is to help make sure that the projects undertaken have a return on investment and are not going to hurt the organization financially. He believes the CEO and CFO sometimes need to take a stand, especially when physicians are involved and want to take the organization in a different direction.

CMIO Role

According to Christopher Barrilleaux, EJGH's CMIO, the CMIO needs to be a leader, cheerleader and salesperson. The CMIO needs to use the system, which means practicing medicine, and be willing to say when the system needs improvement. The CMIO also needs to be willing to tell project sponsors what reality is. "The CMIO needs to say 'We can't do it because it's not for the greater good, or we can't do it because of budgetary reasons,'" says Barrilleaux.

Nurse Executive Role

Janice Kishner, VP and chief nursing executive, believes that the nurse executive needs to be out observing what is actually happening on the floors. What's not working? Is a wireless network working? The governance process is not about waiting for people to come to decision makers. "They can't suggest what they don't know," Kishner says. "We need to be thinking about whether there's a technology answer to the problems we see."

Project Sponsor Role

The project sponsor works with a project manager to prepare a business case and presents that case to the IMSC. After the project is approved, the sponsor is responsible for implementation, working with a project manager.

Physician and Nurse Involvement

Physicians are selected for committees because of both their position and their influence in the organization. Members are not paid for serving on the IMSC or the clinical operations committee. They are paid for serving on the EMRC, an advisory committee consisting only of physicians related to the implementation of the EMR and computerized physician order entry (CPOE). This committee requires many hours of work and attendance at night meetings. The bylaws require that members be paid. Physicians are paid by the hour, but money is a held back to ensure that they attend meetings. Physicians are also paid a per diem when they travel outside the area, for example, to view a Cerner system operating in another city.

Governance and Cerner

Matt MacVey, Cerner's site executive, believes that Cerner needs governance to get decisions made and constrain scope. The scope of a multiyear contract between Cerner and EJGH needs to be turned into a detailed description of what has to be delivered. Meeting Meaningful Use requirements is part of the contract, but the choices for doing so are not specified. Governance needs to contribute information and support. For example, in converting clinics to a Cerner ambulatory care system, how much data should be converted? The answer will affect contract costs. The governance committees need to determine which contract options will work best and help MacVey to describe them.

IT Governance and Project Management
Project Management Supports Governance

After approval, a project charter is prepared. Table 6-2 shows the components of a project charter.

The PMO has created and tracks an idea list of the projects under consideration for which no scope document or business case has been prepared. Preparing the necessary information will be resource intensive but Matt MacVey feels it is important. "If we don't do this, people develop their own set of data about why we should do the project," he says. It is then difficult to persuade them to look at other data.

PMO and Project Portfolio Management

Jim Burton believes that portfolio management is needed because there are interdependencies between projects. It helps make choices on the use of resources. The customer can make choices about how resources are used and see the trade-offs.

The PMO manages all projects, not just those that go through the IMSC review process. There should be a methodology for all projects. The PMO should be contributing to capacity planning.

Cerner operates the PMO and employs the project managers, many of whom have been hospital employees for years. The PMO manages non-Cerner projects. MacVey describes the goal as getting to the point where they resource load all the project plans. They can then roll it up and look at those resources across the entire organization. "We're trying to get to the point where there is a defined time line for proposing a project as part of the budgetary cycle so we can look at the entire portfolio of projects before a decision is made."

Table 6-2: Components for a Project Charter (Document granting organizational authority to the project manager to proceed with the project)

1. What is the project goal, scope, and key deliverables?
2. Who is the project manager?
3. What level of authority does he/she have?
4. Who are the required members of the project team?
5. What are the requirements for success?
6. Next steps for project organization and timeframe.
7. Call for commitment from necessary stakeholders.
8. What are the time expectations (start, finish)?

When the IMSC first approves a project, it is approving the funding, not a specific start date. The CIO comes back to the committee with a time line after reviewing with the PMO the other projects that are being implemented. Burton provides the committee a spreadsheet with information about all the projects and asks for decisions about which ones should proceed and which should be delayed.

Burton believes that "portfolio management is a wasted exercise unless you're within 10 percent of scope." He believes that portfolio management will improve as the discipline of governance is accepted and methodologies are applied. The PMO director is working on that.

Project Manager Role

Project managers help project sponsors develop business cases. They prepare a mini-scope that describes the high-level cost of the project, how long the project will take and the resources required. After the project is approved, they prepare a full-blown scope document. The business sponsor and the department head sign off on the scope.

Project managers then provide the information to keep the project on time and on budget. Comparing projects is not their job.

Keys to Successful IT Governance

Jim Burton believes there are four keys to success:

- **Perseverance and knowing your end goal.** The goal is both a process and an outcome. The process should not be CIO dependent. The CIO should lay out the facts and give an opinion, but not make a decision. The business sponsor has to drive the decision.
- **Communication.** You need to be out there with the customer and not sitting in your office. You are going to have difficult times in governance and you need the personal relationships.
- **Delivering what you promised.** People begin to realize that if they are involved in the governance process, they are going to get results.
- **Having strong leadership at the top.** There is going to be conflict, and the person at the top needs to be able to enforce the governance process. Governance is about trust. If you have people gaming the system and winning approval for their projects, the governance process loses all credibility.

Judy Brown, EJGH's CFO, believes the keys to success are:

- **Encouraging good communication.** Allow everybody to weigh in on what is going to impact the organization the most. IT governance enables all areas of the hospital to weigh in, regardless of whether it is about the revenue cycle, business applications or clinical applications. Proposals then need to be funneled to a single steering committee to decide what is best for the organization, given limited resources. Everybody needs to understand what the strategy of the organization is and how their project affects the organization.

- **Providing a way to handle exceptions.** As described earlier, EJGH has a process for handling immediate needs between meetings of the steering committee.

Christopher Barrilleaux, EJGH's CMIO, adds:
- **Deciding on a process and sticking to it.** Do not allow people to circumvent the IT governance process. People appeal to senior executives to get what they feel they need. Barrilleaux sees that happening less frequently at EJGH. "We've demonstrated that we only have sufficient resources to carry out some projects. If we go out and do everybody's project, nothing gets done," he says.

Janice Kishner, EJGH's VP and chief nursing executive, believes that keys to success must include:
- **Having zero tolerance for bypassing the governance structure.**
- **Supplying enough education and knowledge for the team to understand the governance structure.** Anyone who could propose a project needs to know how information flows and how decisions are made. "We do that by having very visible members of the governance structure attached to our various councils and committees," she says.
- **Providing ongoing feedback about project proposals.** "You have to get back to them after they propose a project. If you don't get back to them, they will find another way to get the project done," Kishner explains.
- **Speaking directly with someone who has tried to go around the process.** The active support of senior management can be especially effective. For example, a manager who finds out that a project reached the IMSC without being reviewed by one of the subcommittees might tell the project's sponsor that future attempts to game the system will not be tolerated. "We need to use those moments for education," Kishner points out.

Matt MacVey adds:
- **Communication and education.** Determine the right level of detail in communication. Do not show bias in communication. If communication is muddy and appears biased, you won't get a decision. Tying the information to the decision that needs to be made is key.

Mistakes to Avoid
Jim Burton believes there are three major mistakes to avoid:
- **Compromising on what is right to make pressure go away.** This dilutes the influence of the CIO. When the CIO is willing to deviate from the process, credibility is lost.
- **Not starting the governance process when you first arrive.** Once the "spigot" of projects has been opened, it is difficult to turn it off. You need to slow down the evaluation process while the governance process develops.

- **Allowing a siloed process that separates physicians, nurses and managers.** When Burton arrived there were too many committees. The process was siloed. Physicians and nurses had separate committees and never met together. There is now a weekly meeting where the CMIO, the CNO, the medical director and the CIO meet to discuss changes related to clinical projects.

Judy Brown believes there are two mistakes to avoid:
- **Make sure that IT does not prioritize projects before they enter the governance process.** Doing so could push projects down that should have a higher priority.
- **Do not let departments, including IT, go around the process.** Try to get IT involved from the beginning. This helps avoid disappointment because people often do not understand the implications of their project in terms of resources and impact on other projects.

Christopher Barrilleaux adds:
- **Remember that the people who do not agree with you are not your enemies.** Bring the people who are the loudest critics into the process.

Matt MacVey adds:
- **Not supplying the right level of data for the decisions that need to be made.** The decision then gets deferred to the next meeting.

Conclusion

Jim Burton believes that IT governance is "50 percent culture." "In an organization that doesn't want to change, nobody wants governance," he says. "Governance means accountability, making decisions and knowing what's going on in your business. You can't point your finger at someone else and say I didn't know. A lot of people say they want it, but many don't want it."

Chapter 7

Case Study: *IT Governance at Eastern Maine Healthcare Systems, Brewer, ME*

Introduction

Eastern Maine Healthcare Systems (EMHS) is a regional healthcare system serving all of central, eastern and northern Maine. EMHS has seven member hospitals and three affiliated hospitals, integrated physician groups, home health organizations, nursing homes and retirement communities, and emergency transport organizations. Its largest hospital is Eastern Maine Medical Center (EMMC), which has 411 acute care beds. The other six member hospitals range in size from 14 to 100 acute care beds.[54] EMMC won HIMSS's Nicholas E. Davies Organizational Award of Excellence in 2008[55] and was named a Most Wired Hospital in 2010 for the third year.[56]

EMHS's vision is to "be the best rural health care system in America by 2012."

EMHS's president and CEO, Michelle Hood, has written on the importance of IT.

> As we address the many challenges of building the next generation's healthcare model, the opportunities to harness the tremendous power of IT cannot and should not be underutilized. We must harvest the capabilities provided through analytics and information exchange in increasingly innovative ways. We can shape proactive responses to market dynamics.[57]

Purpose of IT Governance

Hood believes that the purpose of IT governance is transparency. "The effective engagement of clinical and administrative leaders across the organization in understanding the challenges of IT is key," Hood says. "We need to understand what the competing resource requirements look like and to give everybody as much information as they need so that they have common expectations about how quickly and what scope of IT utilization we expect." She also notes transparency allows for a better understanding of what's going on so as to be more efficient in recommendations regarding everything from what kind of software is needed to how quickly work can be accomplished."

Erik Steele, EMHS's chief medical officer, believes that IT governance provides a way to make decisions about resource allocation. "IT is a constrained resource, and you have to have a way to allow people to have input into resource allocation," Steele explains. "You need to offer real access and real sharing of decision making to members of the organization so there's legitimacy and credibility to the governance process."

Because of the impact the EMR was going to have on physicians at EMHS, Steele believes it was extremely important to have a process for engaging physicians and giving them a place to register their concerns and to share in decision making. "The bottom-line objective is to implement a transformative, system-wide project without 'blowing the place up'—having a revolt," Steele says. "There are varying degrees of that. You can wind up with a medical staff that is alienated for a significant period of time. If you have good governance, the chance of not doing that is much greater."

Cathy Bruno, EMHS's CIO, believes that the purpose of IT governance is to set the priorities for Information Systems (IS) and to ensure that EMHS is getting value from the systems it has. "IS is viewed differently because of the governance process," Bruno says. "We are viewed as trying to do what is best for EMHS and measuring the value."

Alignment with Organization's Strategy
EMHS has defined six strategic pillars and their related goals and objectives. The six strategic pillars are people, quality, service, finance, growth and community.[58] Hood believes alignment is achieved not through the governance process, but by including IT as a component of strategic planning and the process of creating capital and operating budgets. "Projects are no longer seen as IT projects, but strategic projects enabled by IT," she says.

Committee Structure
The EMHS leadership council decided in 2004 to start the Together Project to implement a common set of applications across the entire EMHS system. Bruno realized that a governance process was needed both for the project and to create an IT strategic plan. An IS governance committee was created that is chaired by the CEO. The IS governance committee is appointed by the leadership council, which includes the senior managers of EMHS and the CEOs of member organizations. The members of the IS governance committee have no fixed term. Four of the CEOs of member facilities are currently on the IS governance committee, and there is no defined rotation among the CEOs in the system. Other members of the IS governance committee are the EMHS CMO, CIO, CFO and VP for continuum of care, as well as two hospital nurses and a CMIO. The EMHS board of directors does not have an IS committee.

An IS directors group was also established that includes the IS directors at each member hospital, the EMHS CIO, the CMIO from EMMC, the EMHS directors of customer support, clinical applications, member services, business process support, provider services, enterprise infrastructure, programming and interface, business systems and the PMO. Only two facility IS directors are system employees. The remainder are member employees. The IS directors group provides input on policies and anything that is taken to the IS governance committee. The directors group provides a forum for the IS directors from each facility to discuss common issues, such as the different ways that facilities are handling personal portable devices. They also generate project requests.

There is an additional governance process for eQuest, the initiative to meet Meaningful Use requirements and receive federal stimulus funds. There is a steering committee that is chaired by EMHS's chief medical officer and includes the chief medical officers and chief nursing officers of each organization, the eQuest medical director and nursing director, the CIO, a human resources representative and a physician practice representative. A similar governance process exists for the Bangor Beacon Community grant implementation of care management and the eQuest program (5010, ICD-10, and HIPAA privacy compliance).

There is also a clinical coordinating committee composed of the chief medical officer, the chief nursing officer and the president of the medical staff of each member organization. There is a subcommittee of the clinical coordinating committee that is called the clinical systems steering committee that has been delegated to make design decisions about the EMR, the Cerner Millennium system. There is also a decision support work group composed of physicians that makes decisions on order sets and clinical pathways.

Governance Processes and Workflows

Requests for projects can be made in a number of ways. Physicians and nurses can go online and raise an issue about the EMR and that issue will be tracked until it is resolved, which may result in a project. They can speak personally to the CMO or CMIO at their facility. An individual who wishes to propose a project often goes to the IS director at their hospital, who will then forward it to member services. This includes projects that would require less than 400 hours of IS time (the cutoff used to define a major project). Member services is part of the client care collaborative, which includes member services (which handles new ideas), the PMO (for projects being implemented) and business operations. Revenue cycle projects are handled by the finance department.

When a project request is made, staff from member services interview the proposer to get more detail. They engage in progressive elaboration of the proposal, asking a series of questions to determine both the needs and the scope of the project. Member services does not want to move forward and develop specifications for a project that costs over $1 million when the sponsor was interested in a project that costs $100,000. Member services is also on the lookout for opportunities for collaboration among member organizations and encourages information sharing, joint projects and reharvesting of prior work whenever possible.

If it is a clinical project, the proposal will go to the clinical collaborative. The medical director of eQuest and the nurse who heads the eQuest initiative are the co-chairs of the clinical collaborative, which is an IS multidisciplinary and self-directed staff committee. They will ask if the capability already exists or if the core vendor has a product, explore how the functionality enhances zero defect and quality of care, and develop a plan to encourage provider utilization. EMHS has chosen some system-wide applications, and any time a facility wants to purchase something different they have to ask permission. They estimate what the scale of the project would be. It then goes to the project review committee, which will look at the feasibility of IS doing the work involved. The proposal will then get a project manager, who will begin to provide the details needed for a business case if the project will require more than 400 hours of IS staff time. If it needs less than 400 hours, the proposal will go back to the requesting institution to determine if they want to use their allocation of hours. If the project applies only to their facility, the hardware and software costs would come out of their budget. Ralph Swain, EMHS's corporate director of IS applications, believes that project sponsors rarely ignore this process because they risk being told that the project is not feasible for IS department support.

The project request form is an Excel spreadsheet that asks:
- What is the strategic alignment (relation to the strategic pillars and related goals and objectives)?
- What are the affected or interested business unit and departments within the unit?
- What is the proposed time line and drop-dead date?
- What are the critical and ideal outcomes?
- What related work is already occurring or planned for?
- What is the total labor and capital budget?
- What are the benefits with targets (e.g., increase operating efficiency by 10%) and measures?
- Has a solution been identified and if so, does it replace a system?
- Does it require additional hardware or software?
- Does it require an interface to an existing system?
- Who will be responsible for maintenance?
- Is information contained that would be subject to HIPAA security requirements?
- Is the project discretionary or nondiscretionary?
- Is authorization required from a department head and executive sponsor?

Project Prioritization
In 2006, EMHS began using an annual prioritization process that required the IS governance committee to rank all major projects, defined as those that required more

than 400 hours of IS department staff time. The cutoff of 400 hours was derived by looking at project data and trying to determine what the 80/20 split was. By using 400 hours the committee would be looking at the bigger projects. Business plans were prepared. Projects were ranked on their relationship to the six strategic pillars. After a few years, the committee members decided the process was too grueling, there was too much detail and it was exhausting to spend an entire day doing the ranking. Also, approving and prioritizing proposals to get money from a strategic capital pool was no longer necessary when that pool was eliminated.

The governance committee began allocating IS staff project and work request hours to each member organization. IS staff estimates the available hours for new projects and then allocates them on the basis of the percentage of money contributed by each member facility. EMMC is the largest member hospital and pays approximately 85% of the cost of the system's IS department, so it receives 85% of the hours. If a system that affects all members needs changes (e.g., the replacement of Exchange e-mail servers), the required hours are allocated to facilities and taken from their allotment. The facility decides how the remaining hours are used.

EMHS has, therefore, evolved from a centralized project-prioritization process to a more decentralized process. The creation of business plans for major projects has been kept. The IS governance committee still has to approve major projects, but when they get done depends on member organizations and their budgets.

The allocation process is likely to change because three major initiatives are projected to consume all the available IS staff hours. They are meeting Meaningful Use requirements; conversion to ICD-10 and compliance with the proposed HIPAA Privacy Rule and 5010 transaction standards; and Outreach and Growth, the initiative to meet Pioneer Accountable Care Organization (ACO) requirements. The Centers for Medicare & Medicaid Services (CMS) has approved EMHS for the first round of funding for ACOs. Eric Hartz, EMMC's CMIO and the medical director of the system-wide Meaningful Use initiative, points out that this will require IS resources. "We're going to need to do data mining and profiling of all our patients," Hartz explains. "We'll have to look at physicians and diseases to see what the variations are. What is truly value added and what do we not need to do? What could we do in a different way? We'll have to track approximately 30 quality measures."

The three initiatives are forecasted to consume all the current IS department project resources. Allocation of hours to facilities would have to end, but other projects might be undertaken if resources remain.

Eric Hartz believes the work of the IS governance committee will change and become harder. In the future, it is more likely that a project proposed by an individual facility will be a system project. The governance committee will have to prioritize those projects.

"The facilities are now on a more equal playing field," Hartz says. "The Together Project and compliance with Meaningful Use requirements have moved them to the same place in terms of applications. In the past, EMMC was ahead in implementing applications such as an eICU. EMMC had its own fund of hours so it really didn't need to go to the governance committee. We decided on our own priorities. Now if EMMC wants to do a project, there is a 99% probability it's going to benefit other facilities in the system. New projects all become system projects. The governance committee is now going to have to prioritize them. A few projects will not be applicable to all facilities, for example, those needed for the comprehensive cancer center. But that will be rare."

Hartz continues by asking, "Given all of the mandated initiatives, are we going to find more resources or tell facilities they can't finish projects they feel are important for three years? How will the IS governance committee prioritize projects if resources become available?"

Post-Implementation Review

Hood believes that post-implementation reviews should be done by the operating committee of the sponsor. The IS governance committee has done a post-implementation review of projects a few times, including CPOE and bedside medication verification. There is no rule about which projects should be reviewed. Cathy Bruno believes there would need to be a process of defining—before implementation, what the values are; this is rarely done.

Relation to Budgeting

Each year, Bruno proposes a total IS budget to the CFO, who determines the percentages allocated to each member facility after the board approves the budget. Expenditures related to meeting Meaningful Use requirements are allocated differently. If the facility did not have an application, it is charged on the basis of net patient revenue. So if EMMC had an application, it was not charged again.

Most of the capital spending comes from the budgets of member facilities. Most of the money comes from EMMC. Bruno requests that they include items needed by EMHS in their capital budget. A few items, such as a system-wide e-mail server, are in the EMHS budget. The EMHS board's finance committee approves all capital and operating budgets, including IT spending. There is no separate board oversight review of IT.

Communication

The IS governance committee does not have a representative from every facility. Bruno goes to each member facility and explains what IS is doing and what projects are proposed before each IS governance committee meeting.

Executive Roles
CIO Role
Bruno believes her role is "creating the process and then building the coalitions for its success." She looks at the issues, decides what needs to be solved and then develops proposals. "And then we sell it and modify it as we go around if somebody has a better idea," she says.

Bruno reports to the CMO after the promotion of the CFO to CEO of one of the member organizations. She suggested this arrangement because the CMO has been deeply engaged in integration of IS offerings into zero defect and process improvement projects, a co-sponsor with her on Meaningful Use initiatives and "a wonderful change agent."

Bruno feels she is not giving up authority in creating the governance process. "I have to build a coalition anyway and I'm not all-knowing," she says. "It's very powerful to have an IS governance committee. I can say, 'You have to develop a business plan because the IS governance committee wants it.' The CEO chairs the governance committee. It gives me a lever. It gives me a way to say to the organization there is a process and it is supported by the organization. I don't see how in a complex organization where there are decisions that are conflicting that I could just decide. Our process is very collaborative and results in innovation and a high-performing IS portfolio for our providers and patients."

CEO Role
Hood chairs the IS governance committee. She has said this about clinical IT: "The chief executive officer's accountability must be clearly and visibly attached to these initiatives' expected outcomes. . . . The CEO must take every opportunity to effectively link the investments in clinical IT with the mission of and benefits to the organization."[59]

CMO Role
Steele believes the role of the CMO is to "make it work." "You are the utility infielder and your job is to make it work—whatever that takes," he says. He suggests talking directly to physicians. "Push through a process for tracking concerns and getting them resolved. Good governance isn't a random event."

CMIO Role
EMHS does not have a CMIO. Each member organization has either a CMIO or a physician champion for the Meaningful Use initiative. Hartz, the CMIO at EMMC, also serves in a system-wide role as the medical director of the Meaningful Use initiative. In addition, he serves as an advisor to Bruno and, in his system-wide role, meets monthly with other CMIOs and physicians in the EMHS system. He shares with them what is happening in IS and what he needs help with. Bruno believes that Hartz is "an expert user of clinical decision support and is instrumental in using data to drive process change in each of his roles."

Project Executive Sponsor Role

Project executive sponsors participate in the development of a business plan, present to the IS governance committee, provide linkage to the leadership council, participate in the governance of the project and then work on the implementation of the project. "Most executive sponsors take their responsibility to deliver the project objectives very seriously," Bruno says.

Physician Involvement

Steele believes that to engage physicians and obtain commitment you need to pay them for their time. Physicians who are not employed by EMHS or its members are paid on a per-hour basis. If they are being paid for another role such as medical director, committee time is included in the duties they are compensated for. Physicians who are employed get dedicated time and are not penalized if they are paid partly on productivity.

Erik Steele believes that to keep physicians engaged you need to provide multiple modes of communication. CMIO and Meaningful Use reports are formally on the agenda of medical staff meetings. Reminders are built into the EMR. "You may need to call physicians as well as send materials to emphasize the importance of what they should be reading," he says. "If they miss a meeting, a staff member needs to follow up with them and tell them what happened to issues they care about. Their performance needs to be monitored. If they are not showing up for meetings or repeatedly approving changes that their group later objects to, they need to be approached and asked to change behavior or be replaced."

Hartz notes, "Our philosophy is to flood them with information in every possible way you can think of. We use personal communication, paper and electronic newsletters, and attendance at departmental meetings. We try to make IT part of the agendas."

It is important that physicians understand the needs of a healthcare system and not just an individual facility or specialty. Steele believes, "To get physicians to think about representing the system rather than their individual facilities or specialties, we try to set expectations. For example, we told physicians that there will be system-wide formulary. We are doing that as a group."

Hartz points out to physicians where information is available on patients across the system because of IS. "It's more efficient, you don't have to duplicate services," he says. "We frame it in terms of patient safety, quality and efficiency. So they buy into it." He points out that Maine's health information exchange will improve care by allowing access to records from physicians who are not in the EMHS system.

IT Governance and Project Management
PMO and Project Portfolio Management

The project management office (PMO) is part of what is called the client care collaborative, which also includes business operations and member services. The PMO is responsible for projects that are being implemented. Member services is responsible for managing project ideas or requests, leading customer service advocacy, encouraging collaboration among member organizations and intervening when customer expectations are not being met. In regard to governance, business operations is responsible for data acquisition and reporting on the operations of the IS department, including reporting to the IT governance committee. Project status reports are prepared and disseminated by the PMO.

DAPTIV is the project and portfolio management tool used by EMHS (www.daptiv .com). It is used to track the three portfolios. The discovery portfolio contains ideas for projects. The business portfolio includes projects that are being implemented. The foundation portfolio includes the support projects that maintain the current systems. The items in the discovery portfolio are tracked to determine if member ideas have moved to the next stage or whether there is a need to discuss what happened.

Mistakes to Avoid

Members of the EMHS team have several suggestions on things to avoid when developing an IT governance process.

- **Providing too much information.** Hood believes it is a mistake to provide too much detailed information to people involved in governance. Information needs to be filtered. Providing too much information puts them in the role of management. "It's a fine line, though," she cautions. "They should be involved in issues like Meaningful Use and the use of informatics to support new care delivery systems."
- **Taking criticism personally.** Bruno believes you shouldn't express frustration and take criticism personally. "You need to engage your constituents in a positive way," she says.
- **Lacking a clear process for IT funding or having poor staff support.** Steele believes that having an unclear process for defining how much money IT gets is a mistake. "If there is a lot of variability so that IT gets less money during the year, the IT governance process is degraded and the confidence of the IT governance members is degraded," Steele says. He believes that inadequate staff support for IT governance is also a mistake. "Good background information is needed well in advance. Good minutes that are action oriented are needed to provide credibility," he says.

Keys to Successful IT Governance

Bruno believes the keys to successful IT governance are:

- **Aligning what you are doing with the organization.** "You want to make sure your process supports your organization's overall goals and strategic plan," she says. "You have to include the organizations goals and strategies in the process, for example, in the business plan."
- **Aligning with the culture of the organization.** "You can be out in front too far," Bruno says. "I've tried to be out in front in developing the process, for example, in requiring business plans. I try to listen to their feedback. We've decentralized some of the decision making but now are in the process of moving toward greater centralization. The incentive program for Meaningful Use has greatly increased the degree to which we work together."
- **Transparency.** "Being really clear and communicating a lot is key," Bruno says. "Build relationships and make sure they know what you're doing and what your decision processes are. There shouldn't be any surprises."

Erik Steele believes the keys to success are:

- **Being good at estimating the number of hours required for project implementation.** IT governance members can then determine priorities. If you do not have good estimating skills, you are just guessing.
- **A committee structure that provides a place for issues to be resolved.** For example, the clinical systems steering committee deals with the EMR components of the Millennium product.
- **The personal investment of the chief medical officer in the process.** The CMO has to understand how decisions are made. CMOs have to make sure that issues get tracked and resolved. The loop has to be closed back to the initiating physician. The CMIO, the CIO and the CMO have to be partners. The CMO needs to be involved in key discussions to make sure that the physician perspective is represented. "You have to make sure the physician's voice is effective in decision making," Steele says.
- **Transparency.** Physicians want to know how decisions are made. They want some processes embedded in policy. Physicians and nurses can go online and raise an issue about the EMR and that issue will be tracked until it is resolved. Others will go to the CMIO and CMO and raise the concern directly.

Hartz believes the keys to success are:

- **Having a clear process for presenting projects to the governance committee.** It is important to define the criteria for determining if a project should go forward. Equally important is giving the participants in the system some guidance on the amount of work they should be pushing up to the governance committee. "The governance committee should have an overall vision of how the pieces are going to fit together and advise the individual entities on what they're supposed to do," Hartz says.

Conclusion

Michelle Hood believes that "IT governance is dynamic and needs to change as the organization becomes more mature and people have increasing understanding and confidence in the process. "We've evolved in governance from being too detail-oriented to becoming more strategic," she says.

Hood sees EMHS as a hybrid. "Certain things are very much standardized and decided at the system level. For example, my office is responsible for hiring all affiliate CEOs. We've retained local boards because they are the links to their communities," she explains. "We're moving toward more standardized and more integrated decision making. This is because we're moving toward clinical integration quickly. We run an eICU from one location, for example. That's going to affect IT."

Chapter 8

Case Study: *IT Governance at Saint Luke's Health System, Kansas City, MO*

Introduction

Saint Luke's Health System is a faith-based, not-for-profit health system that operates 11 hospitals and related healthcare services in the Kansas City metropolitan area and surrounding region. In 2007, Saint Luke's celebrated the 125th year of its flagship hospital, Saint Luke's Hospital of Kansas City. In 2011, it won the Most Wired Award from *Hospitals and Health Networks* magazine for using Internet-based technologies to connect with patients, physicians and nurses, employees, suppliers and health plans (www.saintlukeshealthsystem.org).

Purpose of IT Governance

According to Deborah Gash, Saint Luke's vice president and CIO, the purpose of IT governance is alignment with the business strategy of the organization. It should ensure that the business leaders have a sense of accountability for what is happening in IT and dispel the idea that IT projects only affect IT.

George Pagels, chief medical officer of Saint Luke's Health System and chief executive officer of Saint Luke's East, views IT now as a service provided to clinicians as opposed to a product provided by a department that dictated how things got done because they had the technology. "Historically in this organization, IT decided what they thought we needed as clinicians and provided it and configured it," Pagels says. "There was a real disconnect. That has changed."

Carl Dirks, Saint Luke's CMIO, believes that the primary purpose of IT governance is to ensure that clinicians are having their needs met and are supported by the IT investments being made.

Alignment with Organization's Strategy

The calendar for IT governance is tied to the strategic planning process of the organization. The document that describes IT governance begins by describing how the IT strategic plan is created. IT governance is not focused only on the capital budgeting process. According to Gash, you have to define first what you want to accomplish and then develop a budget to support it. "The organization defines a specific amount of money they want to spend on IT, and then the question is how it should be spent to support a strategy," she says.

Dirks believes that IT governance improves alignment by creating transparency. There are strong lines of communication and transparency about which projects are being worked on and the prioritization of projects. It is also clear what resources are available, including human capital. There is a direct feedback process for clinicians into the prioritization and optimization of the systems and processes being implemented.

Sponsors must say how the implementation of an IT project will improve four goals of the organization: patient safety, practice efficiency, customer/employee satisfaction and financial stability. These are used as criteria for prioritization.

Committee Structure

Saint Luke's management committee is the leadership body of the organization that also serves as the senior governance body for IT. The members of the management committee are the system CEO, CFO, CMO, CNO and CIO. Also included are the CEOs of each Saint Luke's facility and the VPs of human resources, risk management and compliance, marketing, business development and public affairs.

This group is supported by clinical and business groups that prioritize projects. The management committee determines the allocation of funding between the two groups. Gash notes, "We have a flat organization, and the people who run the management committee would typically also be on the IT steering committee." The management committee has delegated some of the decision making about what is critical to the organization to prioritization groups. "These committees, therefore, perform one of the functions of a steering committee. There is no board of directors committee for IT," she adds.

Prioritization Committees

The clinical applications prioritization group is comprised of:
- One physician representative from each metropolitan facility, as appointed by the medical executive board of the respective facility, with input from the CMO, for a term of three years
- The chief nursing officers from each of the metro facilities and the system CNO
- The CMO
- The CMIO (ex officio)
- A senior IT representative (ex officio)
- The corporate controller (ex officio)

The chair of the committee is the CMO. The clinical applications prioritization group meets once or twice a year. Pagels asks the medical staff executive committee of each facility to name a physician to serve. "I encourage them not to recommend an IT-oriented person but a clinician who can provide a clinical point of view. It's been a really good process," Pagels says.

The business applications prioritization group is comprised of:
- Representatives from system entities and key system process leaders, as appointed by senior VP/CFO of Saint Luke's Health System for a term of three years. This includes chief financial officers and department heads from finance, patient accounting, health information management and ancillary departments.
- The CMO
- The CMIO (ex officio)
- A senior IT representative (ex officio)
- The corporate controller (ex officio)

The chair of this committee is appointed by the VP/CFO. In both prioritization groups, the IT representative does not have a vote.

Information Technology Users Group (ITUG)

The information technology users group (ITUG) is comprised of representatives from each of the metropolitan Saint Luke's facilities, as well as key system-level functions (e.g., marketing, business research and development), as appointed by the executive management teams of each facility or Saint Luke's Health System area. Also included is a senior representative from the information services department, the CMIO and the corporate controller. The membership is expected to represent a balance of clinical and operations perspectives, including but not limited to, nursing, laboratory, radiology/imaging, pharmacy, materials management, health information management, human resources, home health and finance. Members hold appointments for a period of three years, with one-third of the membership rotating off each year. A chair is appointed by the management committee and is responsible to the chairs of the clinical and business applications prioritization groups. ITUG is currently co-chaired by the CIO and the VP of healthcare informatics.

ITUG meets to discuss implementation and how clinical and business applications are affecting each other. ITUG is expected to resolve operational issues that might affect an in-process project schedule or budget and to communicate operational issues with in-process or production systems that might improve patient safety, reduce medical errors or improve operational efficiencies.

Governance Processes and Workflows

Saint Luke's holds an annual half-day executive planning retreat that is attended by all business unit operating executive officers (hospitals, medical group and alternative care businesses) and corporate leaders (CEO, CFO, CMO, CIO, HR, planning, etc.).

The session is chaired by the system CEO, SVP of strategic planning and CFO. The objective is to set priorities for the year, determine available capital and operating funding, provide education on industry developments and define which major initiatives will receive funding.

After the system strategic plan is developed, the CIO leads an effort to update the IT five-year strategic plan. The plan sets measurable three- to five-year goals and objectives that are necessary to achieve the desired future. The goals and objectives are structured in three areas: clinical, financial/administrative and infrastructure. The goals and objectives are linked to the five perspectives of a Balanced Scorecard: workforce availability, customer, growth, quality and financial.

The two prioritization groups appointed by the management committee evaluate project requests, rank the requests and present recommendations to the management committee along with the updated IT five-year plan and budget. Three additional quarterly two-hour sessions are held throughout the year (as part of a regularly scheduled management committee session) to gauge progress, discuss issues and make course corrections as needed related to funding, resources or scope of IT initiatives.

Updates to the strategic plan are given to the management committee, the prioritization groups and ITUG so they all understand the current status of IT projects by looking at consistent information. Saint Luke's has not separated the new-project approval process from the review of current projects and the budgeting of IT operations.

The management committee receives the list of prioritized projects as well as a list of current projects and the growth and replacement needs of IT at the same time. An example is the replacement of the radiology system, which was prioritized knowing it would be several years before it was implemented, as other projects had to be completed first.

Policies and Procedures
The CIO solicits requests for new IT projects approximately 90 days prior to when the IT capital budget is due. To present a project proposal to a prioritization committee the project sponsor must follow specific guidelines:
- A business plan is required.
- There must be agreement among peers that the project is important. If it is a system-wide project, the sponsor has to have gotten the approval of relevant people from other facilities. For example, to propose a system-wide radiology project, the head of radiology at one facility must obtain approval from all the other radiology department heads. The cost gets allocated to all facilities.
- The project must have an executive sponsor—someone who is on the management committee.
- There must be staff available in the department to do the work involved.

Table 8-1 shows the contents of the IT prioritization request worksheet, which asks for:
- A description of the project
- Five-year capital costs
- Five-year operational costs
- Projected operating cost savings (including FTEs)
- Resource estimate for project completion
- Project justification and linkage to strategic plan
- Administrator approval

The CIO or someone on her staff works with project sponsors to consider what the best application would be. Saint Luke's has adopted a core vendor strategy and has selected McKesson as the preferred vendor. So the first question is whether there is a McKesson application that could be used. IT staff will help sponsors refine their business cases and shop, if necessary, for an application. The sponsor takes the lead in writing a business case. IT staff will also define the infrastructure and integration needed and the IT staff hours required. IT staff review the requests to ensure that the IT cost estimates and technical requirements are understood and not over- or underinflated. The corporate controller reviews the financial projections and agrees or disagrees with them. Requests are then compiled and delivered one week in advance to the prioritization group members for review prior to the meeting to discuss requests.

The IT department also looks for IT solutions to problems that have been identified and examines new technologies to see how they could be applied. If a project would benefit clinical care or business services, the CIO takes it to the relevant customer. This results in action plans for implementing technology. A business case for technology is prepared and taken to the prioritization committees. Gash is the executive sponsor for IT infrastructure projects. Requests related to IT infrastructure are sent to the administrative group and are prioritized along with all other projects.

Projects submitted to IT that are required to meet regulatory requirements or to support ongoing project continuance and construction are not presented to the prioritization groups. This is to ensure that projects required to sustain existing applications and meet external requirements have IT human resources assigned and take priority over new projects.

Gash says that the frequency of attempts to go around the governance process has decreased, "The leadership understands what the process is and they will stop it" she says. Pagels agrees, noting it is because "the process we have works and people feel comfortable with the results."

Table 8-1: Saint Luke's Health System—
Contents of the IT Prioritization Request Worksheet

Saint Luke's Health System - IT Prioritization Request Worksheet
Project Name: Prepared By: Administrator Who Authorizes: Solution Vendor:
Does this request replace existing technology or is it new? Does a new regulation or requirement exist for this request? Is this request for a patient care/biomedical device? Entities included in request
Please give a general description using layman's terms of what the project request encompasses.
Describe the linkage to the SLHS Strategic Action Plan, Achieving Meaningful Use, or to an Entity or Process Scorecard.
What resources will be required to complete this project and if there are any dependencies on other projects.
Describe how the implementation of this project will improve Patient Safety.
Describe how the implementation of this project will improve Practice Efficiency.
Describe how the implementation of this project will improve Customer/Employee Satisfaction.
Describe how the implementation of this project will improve Financial Stability.
Investment Summary
Information Technology Costs
<u>Start Up Costs</u> Hardware Software Implementation Services Consulting/Temporary Help Other
<u>Annual Costs</u> Salary Subscription Fees Annual Maintenance Upgrade Costs Other
Total IT 5 Year Costs:

Table 8-1: (continued)

Non-Information Technology Costs
<u>Start Up Costs</u> Peripheral Equipment Construction Other
<u>Annual Costs</u> Salary Other
Total Non-IT 5 Year Costs:
Revenue Enhancements/Cost Saving Opportunities (Annual)
Increased Revenue Salary Reductions Other Expense Reductions
Total 5 Year Increased Margin:
Start Up Effort (Labor Costs)
Information Technology Non-Information Technology End User Staff Training
Total Start Up Effort:
Total 5 Year Cost (Benefit) for Project:

Project Prioritization

The prioritization committee members are proxies for the management committee. The prioritization process is delegated to them. The clinical applications prioritization group is expected to consider patient safety and practice efficiency. The business applications prioritization group is expected to consider customer/employee satisfaction and financial stability. Will a project generate money or cut costs? The prioritization groups should not be concerned about whether a project will need an enterprise application from McKesson or how difficult the application will be to implement.

If more than 15 requests are submitted to either group, a multi-vote process is used to select the top 15 projects. Then, a matrix is used to rank each project against every other project. The following scale is used:

- Exceedingly more important (score = 10)
- Significantly more important (score = 5)
- No more important (score = 1)
- Significantly less important (score = .1)
- Exceedingly less important (score = .01)

This rating is done twice to produce a smaller list of projects. The prioritization committees do not rank and forward all projects to the management committee. They have rejected projects.

The CIO and her staff try to de-emphasize financial return on investment and how difficult the project will be for IT to implement when they ask the clinical prioritization group to prioritize a project. They want them to focus on the value of the project. The group has the financial numbers, but the discussion tends to be about value. Having the numbers on the request form, however, makes the project sponsor address the question of cost and return at an early stage.

If a project affects only one facility, it is not sent to the prioritization committees. Instead, that facility will pay for the project from its own funds.

In the final days before the budget is due, finance provides budget targets for expenses and capital for the next budget cycle. Using the budget targets, IT leadership works to draw the line at what will be initially submitted to the management committee for inclusion in the next year's IT capital budget. Effort is made to ensure not only that sufficient capital and operating funds will be available but also that sufficient IT staff will be available to implement the projects.

One of the benefits of a five-year plan and the prioritization process is that projects can be started as resources become available. Gash explains, "We have a prioritized list of projects so as resources become available during the year, I'm able to go down the list and begin another project without further approval."

Communication with Physicians

There is a physician leadership group made up of the medical staff officers from each facility. The group meets four or five times a year, and CEOs come as well. The CMIO gives quarterly updates. Pagels is the chair. He points out that the group has oversight of the clinical prioritization process. "The clinical prioritization committee is actually the management committee of this larger group that has delegated the prioritization process," he explains. "The physician leadership group gets the results of the clinical prioritization process and decides whether it agrees with it. All they get is a list of prioritized applications, and the CMIO discusses each one. They haven't challenged the list in the last few years."

There is also a medical informatics committee at the system's largest hospital, Saint Luke's Kansas City, composed of physicians who practice there and at other Saint Luke's facilities. They have no formal decision-making authority but provide feedback and suggestions on the performance of clinical applications.

Post-Implementation Review

There is no requirement for projects to be reviewed after implementation to determine whether the benefits have been received. Some projects have been reviewed, but size was not the primary determining factor. It was the magnitude of the change involved. The project sponsor is the one who must present the results to the management committee.

Relation to Budgeting

Gash is told what the IT budget for capital is for the next five years. After the prioritization process, she determines when projects will be done taking into consideration that money that has been budgeted. She brings this list to the management committee, and they have the opportunity to change the list and begin some projects sooner. They can also decide to go to the finance committee to request more money to get more projects done. The list of projects to be done determines the operating budget. The management committee approves any increases in the operating budget. If the impact is too great on the operating budget, some projects in the capital budget may be postponed. The management committee takes the entire system's capital budget to the board. There is no separate presentation for IT.

Executive Roles
CIO Role

The CIO is a member of the management committee and facilitates and coordinates the prioritization process to ensure that IT aligns with strategic goals of the organization. In addition, the CIO is responsible for execution of the IT plan and seeks feedback and input from operational and clinical leaders.

CEO and CFO Roles

The system CEO and CFO are both members of the management committee that functions as the governing committee for IT.

CMO Role

The CMO is a member of the management committee, chairs the clinical applications prioritization group and also is a member of the business applications prioritization group.

Pagels believes the role of the CMO is to make sure that the process is favorable to the practice of medicine. "To make IT a tool that clinicians drive, rather than the tool driving them, we need to get the right tools at the right time and make sure they're configured correctly."

CMIO Role

The CMIO reports to the system CMO and not to the CIO. Dirks has no direct operational control over IT and does not supervise any of the IT staff involved in implementation, for example, CPOE implementation.

The CMIO co-chairs ITUG and is a member of both the clinical applications and business services prioritization groups but is not a member of the system management committee. This provides the CMIO the opportunity to discuss and vote on both types of applications before they are sent to the management committee. Dirks notes that most applications, with a few exceptions such as revenue cycle management, affect clinical care.

Dirks says, "I am a strategic advisor to the organization. My job description includes closely partnering with the information technology department to successfully manage and implement our clinical IT systems. I closely focus on implementation from the end-user's point of view. That includes closely monitoring implementation down to the level of identifying users who are struggling."

Nurse Executive Role

The system's chief nursing officer is a member of the management committee and the clinical applications prioritization group. The CNOs of each of the facilities are also members of the clinical applications prioritization group.

IT Governance and Project Management
How Project Management Supports Governance

If a project is included in the IT five-year plan, success measures are identified, a timeline for deployment is developed and a customer sponsor and an IT project manager are named to oversee progress in deployment. Action plans, including coordination of resources, are developed in accordance with an IT project management methodology. The project is then reported on and tracked. The current status of all projects is available on an intranet. This includes major milestones of each project.

Action plans are prepared and reviewed quarterly by IT staff. There is a document that lists all of the projects that will be undertaken that year. The CIO meets with IT staff and presents a plan for the next quarter for completing the projects. If projects are not on target, a plan is presented to get back on target. That information is shared with the various user groups.

Todd Hatton is Saint Luke's chief applications officer. In that role, he is responsible for the operation of all existing and new applications. His team includes the program managers, project managers and analysts that actually implement the application with the vendors and customers. He is a member of both the clinical applications and business applications prioritization groups, but he has no vote.

As Hatton points out, "We use the principles of the PMO but we don't have a formal PMO." His division has program managers assigned to each customer segment, such as clinicals and finance. The program managers are responsible for all applications in their areas. Each program manager supervises a group of project managers who have a staff of analysts. Each unit does the application support as well as the implementation for new projects. "We have not split the teams so that one unit does only production support and another does new projects," he says. "A project manager could be supporting an existing application while working on a new project. That approach makes it very clear who the owner of an application is. The customer knows who to go to."

IT has developed a project management methodology. Analysts and project managers are taught project management skills such as the meaning of lag time and how to develop a scope document. The staff are experts in the applications they support. "We don't have the project management mentor role—an individual who helps teach others how to do project management."

Keys to Successful IT Governance

Gash believes the keys to successful IT governance are:
- **Engagement with the leaders of the organization and getting them involved not only in planning but also in executing.** "We have executive sponsors for all of our projects," Gash notes. "They do a lot of the reporting to the board and senior leadership. It has to be someone who is on the management committee. That person can designate a project sponsor from the relevant department."
- **Recognizing that transparency is important.** Everyone should know how the governance process operates, and senior managers communicate that. For example, the CMIO can be viewed as a marketing person for IT, explaining decisions physician to physician.
- **Guidelines for making decisions.** These are defined by the management committee and the board. An example is commitment to a single-vendor strategy rather than best-of-breed.

Pagels believes the keys are:
- **Inclusive prioritization.** Physicians and chief nursing officers must have input into the prioritization of applications. "Physicians need to feel they are just as important as the business side," Pagels says.
- **Involving physicians in configuration.** When the applications are configured, clinicians should have a lot of input. If there are templates, physicians need to know what they are, agree that they will be functional and have significant input on configuration.

Dirks believes a key to success is:
- **A deep and productive working relationship with leadership in the IT department.** He believes he has the ability to affect change on behalf of the clinical mem-

bership and engage them in a productive manner. Clinicians need to know what the objectives are and the reasons behind them.

Gloria Solis, CNO at Saint Luke's East and a member of the ITUG and clinical applications prioritization group, believes one key is:

- **Trust and strong communication.** "Nurses have to trust that I will be carrying their message forward," Solis says. "They have to trust the governance structure. Trust is built by 'walking the walk.'" Solis does not make decisions alone and is inclusive in getting suggestions. "It is important to recognize that there are going to be mistakes and be willing to admit them to users," she adds.

Mistakes to Avoid

Pagels believes it is a mistake not to prioritize against objective criteria. "Good prioritization is comparing every application to every other application according to the same criteria," he says. "If the criterion is patient safety, then every application needs to be compared on that. That's hard work, but if you do that you wind up with something that has face validity. It's acceptable to everyone."

Dirks believes it is a mistake not to obtain strong feedback from your constituents. For the CMIO the constituents are physicians and nurses. "You need to know what people are thinking in order to gain their acceptance and understanding of the changes that are occurring," he points out.

References

1. Weill P, Ross JW. *IT Governance: How Top Performers Manage IT Decision Rights for Superior Results.* Boston: Harvard Business School Press; 2004:vii.

2. Weill P, Ross JW. *IT Governance: How Top Performers Manage IT Decision Rights for Superior Results.* Boston: Harvard Business School Press; 2004:2.

3. Weill P, Ross JW. Don't just lead, govern: how top performing firms manage IT. *MIS Quarterly Executive.* 2004; 3(1):1-17.

4. Schwartz KD. IT governance definition and solutions. CIO Web site. http://www. cio.com/article/111700/IT_Governance_Definition_and_Solutions#what. Published May 22, 2007. Accessed 1/5/2012.

5. Whittingham I. A plain guide to governance. Gantthead Web site. http://www. gantthead.com/content/articles/243476.cfm. Published June 30, 2008. Accessed January 5, 2012.

6. Peterson R. Crafting information technology governance. *Information Systems Management.* Fall 2004:7-22.

7. Thompson D, Johnston P. A benefits-driven approach to IT implementation, Part 2. Healthcare's Most Wired Web site. http://www.hhnmostwired.com/ hhnmostwired_app/jsp/articledisplay.jsp?dcrpath=HHNMOSTWIRED/ Article/data/Spring2008/080709MW_Online_Thompson. Published July 9, 2008. Accessed January 5, 2012.

8. Weill P, Ross JW. *IT Governance: How Top Performers Manage IT Decision Rights for Superior Results.* Boston: Harvard Business School Press; 2004:10.

9. IT Governance Institute. *Board Briefing on IT Governance.* 2nd ed. Rolling Meadows, IL: ISACA; 2003:27. http://www.isaca.org/Knowledge-Center/ Research/Documents/BoardBriefing/26904_Board_Briefing_final.pdf.

10. Weill P, Ross JW. *IT Governance: How Top Performers Manage IT Decision Rights for Superior Results.* Boston: Harvard Business School Press; 2004:10-11.

11. EMHS Abbreviated Strategic Plan. http://www.emh.org.

12. Langabeer J, Delgado R, Mikhail O. Technology governance strategies for maximizing healthcare economic value. *Journal of Healthcare Information Management.* Fall 2007:19-24.

13. ISACA. *Implementing and Continually Improving IT Governance.* Rolling Meadows, IL: ISACA, 2009.

14. ISACA. *Implementing and Continually Improving IT Governance.* Rolling Meadows, IL: ISACA, 2009.

15. ISACA. *Implementing and Continually Improving IT Governance.* Rolling Meadows, IL: ISACA, 2009.

16. ISACA. *Implementing and Continually Improving IT Governance.* Rolling Meadows, IL: ISACA, 2009.

17. Herman D, Scalzi G, Kropf R. Managing Healthcare IS Supply and Demand. Aspen Advisors Web site. www.aspenadvisors.net/results/whitepaper/managing-healthcare-supply-and-demand. Posted June 2011. Accessed July 27, 2011.

18. Meyer ND. Systemic IS governance: an introduction. *Information Systems Management.* Fall 2004:34.

19. Meyer ND. Systemic IS governance: an introduction. *Information Systems Management.* Fall 2004:24.

20. Meyer ND. Systemic IS governance: an introduction. *Information Systems Management.* Fall 2004:24.

21. Meyer ND. Systemic IS governance: an introduction. *Information Systems Management.* Fall 2004:27.

22. Meyer ND. Systemic IS governance: an introduction. *Information Systems Management.* Fall 2004:27.

23. Meyer ND. Systemic IS governance: an introduction. *Information Systems Management.* Fall 2004:29.

24. Weill P, Ross JW. *IT Governance: How Top Performers Manage IT Decision Rights for Superior Results.* Boston: Harvard Business School Press; 2004:2.

25. Meyer ND. Systemic IS governance: an introduction. *Information Systems Management.* Fall 2004:33.

26. Rau KG. Effective governance of IT: design objectives, roles, and relationships. *Information Systems Management.* Fall 2004:35-42.

27. Rau KG. Effective governance of IT: design objectives, roles, and relationships. *Information Systems Management.* Fall 2004:40.

28. Rau KG. Effective governance of IT: design objectives, roles, and relationships. *Information Systems Management.* Fall 2004:41.

29. Weill P, Ross JW. *IT Governance: How Top Performers Manage IT Decision Rights for Superior Results.* Boston: Harvard Business School Press; 2004:222.

30. IT Governance Institute. *Board Briefing on IT Governance.* 2nd Ed. Rolling Meadows, IL: ISACA; 2003:50-52. www.isaca.org/Knowledge-Center/Research/Documents/BoardBriefing/26904_Board_Briefing_final.pdf.

31. Weill P, Ross JW. *IT Governance: How Top Performers Manage IT Decision Rights for Superior Results.* Boston: Harvard Business School Press; 2004:228.

32. Weill P, Ross JW. *IT Governance: How Top Performers Manage IT Decision Rights for Superior Results.* Boston: Harvard Business School Press; 2004:226.

33. Weill P, Ross JW. *IT Governance: How Top Performers Manage IT Decision Rights for Superior Results.* Boston: Harvard Business School Press; 2004:119.

34. Weill P, Ross JW. *IT Governance: How Top Performers Manage IT Decision Rights for Superior Results.* Boston: Harvard Business School Press; 2004:216.

35. Weill P, Ross JW. *IT Governance: How Top Performers Manage IT Decision Rights for Superior Results.* Boston: Harvard Business School Press; 2004:217.

36. Weill P, Ross JW. *IT Governance: How Top Performers Manage IT Decision Rights for Superior Results.* Boston: Harvard Business School Press; 2004:217.

37. Weill P, Ross JW. *IT Governance: How Top Performers Manage IT Decision Rights for Superior Results.* Boston: Harvard Business School Press; 2004:218.

38. Weill P, Ross JW. *IT Governance: How Top Performers Manage IT Decision Rights for Superior Results.* Boston: Harvard Business School Press; 2004:218.

39. Weill P, Ross JW. *IT Governance: How Top Performers Manage IT Decision Rights for Superior Results.* Boston: Harvard Business School Press; 2004:219.

40. Weill P, Ross JW. *IT Governance: How Top Performers Manage IT Decision Rights for Superior Results.* Boston: Harvard Business School Press; 2004:219-220.

41. Kraatz A, Lyons C, Tomkinson J. Strategy and governance for successful implementation of an enterprise-wide ambulatory EMR. *JHIM.* Spring 2010:37.

42. Meyer ND. Systemic IS governance: an introduction. *Information Systems Management.* Fall 2004:25.

43. Meyer ND. Systemic IS governance: an introduction. *Information Systems Management.* Fall 2004:26

44. Weider W. Project governance. Candid CIO blog. http://candidcio.com/2007/08/03/project-governance/. Posted August 3, 2007. Accessed January 6, 2012.

45. Rau KG. Effective governance of IT: design objectives, roles, and relationships. *Information Systems Management.* Fall 2004:35-42.

46. Halamka J. The year of governance. Life as a healthcare CIO blog. http://geekdoctor.blogspot.com/2010/10/year-of-governance.html. Posted October 20, 2010. Accessed July 27, 2011.

47. EMHS Abbreviated Strategic Plan. www.emh.org.

48. Information Systems Audit and Control Association. COBIT framework for governance and control. ISACA Web site. http://www.isaca.org/Knowledge-Center/COBIT/Pages/Overview.aspx. Accessed January 6, 2012.

49. Information Technology Infrastructure Library (ITIL). http://www.itil-officialsite.com/home/home.asp. Accessed January 6, 2012.

50. IT Governance Institute. COBIT 4.1. Rolling Meadows, IL: ISACA; 2003: 31.

51. IT Governance Institute. COBIT 4.1. Rolling Meadows, IL: ISACA; 2003: 22

52. IT Governance Institute. COBIT 4.1. Rolling Meadows, IL: ISACA; 2003: 22

53. IT Governance Institute. COBIT 4.1. Rolling Meadows, IL: ISACA; 2003: 23

54. Maine Hospital Association. Available at www.themha.org/members/hospitalsbysize.htm. Accessed January 16, 2012.

55. EMMC Nicolas E. Davies Organizational Award of Excellence Application. Available at www.himss.org/davies/docs/Organizational/EasternMaineMedical_application.pdf. Accessed January 16, 2012.

56. Most Wired Hospital Award. Available at www.hhnmostwired.com/hhnmostwired/html/winners2010.html. Accessed January 16, 2012.

57. Hood MM. How CEOs drive the clinical transformation and information technology agenda. *Frontiers of Health Services Management*. 2011; 28(1): 15-23.

58. EMHS Abbreviated Strategic Plan. http://www.emh.org.

59. Hood MM. How CEOs drive the clinical transformation and information technology agenda. *Frontiers of Health Services Management*. 2011; 28(1): 15-23.

Index

"f" next to page number denotes a Figure
"t" next to page number denotes a Table

9780984457786

T - #0027 - 220420 - C0 - 229/152/6 - PB - 9780984457786